#STICKWITHMEKID

"HOW TO BUILD AN EMPIRE FROM YOUR BROTHER'S GIRLFRIEND'S MOTHER'S BASEMENT"

ISAAC DANNA

Edited by
ROSE WOLFE

BOOKS

This publication is designed to provide competent and reliable information regarding the subject matter covered. However, it is sold with the understanding that the author and publisher are not engaged in rendering legal, financial, or other professional advice. Laws and practices often vary from state to state and if legal or other expert assistance is required, the services of a professional should be sought. The author and publisher specifically disclaim any liability that is incurred from the use or application of the contents of this book.

A WORD TO MY "DIGITAL MENTORS"

Tai Lopez

You completely changed my life with your "67 Steps Program." I don't even know where to begin. You taught me how to use my own story and create a profitable business around it. Your pillars of success really resonated with how I wanted to balance my life.

Robert Kiyosaki

"Rich Dad, Poor Dad," transformed my outlook on money. You taught me the difference between "assets" and "liabilities." It's my favorite book and the first book I share.

Gary Vaynerchuck

You just motivate me dude. You're way of speaking, in such a blunt and honest way has allowed me to be more expressive without caring about offending someone's feelings.

∾

Grant Cardone

You taught me how to think big and 10X my goals. Your "Millionaire Booklet" and the math to a million dollars created a foundation for my pricing strategies.

Sam Ovens

You taught me how to niche down and how to use my skills to solve problems for businesses. You gave me the confidence to switch my business plan to recurring revenue services and products, only.

Tim Ferriss

Your podcast and your love for conversation and learning has helped me tune into my strengths.

Russell Brunson

Thank you for ClickFunnels and Marketing Secrets.

❧

Armin Van Buuren

A State Of Trance has changed the way I listen to music. It gives me something to look forward to. It's something I can rely on when I'm down. Thank you.

Above & Beyond

Group Therapy has helped me write this book and it's helped me focus throughout my long entrepreneurial work days.

❧

THANKS GOES OUT TO

Luke Younger
Melissa Cote
Patricia Danna or Momma Dukes
John Danna or Papa Dukes
Brittany Mozeak
Rose Wolfe

"Stick With Me, Kid. You'll Go Places!"

— **DOMINIC DANNA** "THE GREAT WHITE HUNTER"

TABLE OF CONTENTS

WHAT TO EXPECT

Alright, from this point forward things start to get a little crazy. I'm giving you a heads up. The reason I say this is because my brain is so all over the place all the time, and I haven't been able to sit down for two weeks straight and just write. I am writing this book when I can, putting time aside as often as I can, and because of this, there are scattered stories and life lessons that I hope will benefit you by reading them. I hope you don't mind.

In my experience, listening to or reading about other people's stories can be one of the best ways to learn. I genuinely don't know how else to write down what I'm thinking. Every time I switch locations and find time to sit and type this up, the new location or new experiences leading up to writing change what I want to say, and how I want to start. Would you agree that if you got value from this book and found a couple of gold nuggets, it would be worth the money, time, and effort you are putting aside? I think so. I have read some pretty ridiculous books, but grabbed a nugget or two and ran. That's my aspiration with this book. I want to deliver as much value as I possibly can. I truly hope that my life lessons, failures, and successes help you navigate your own path before you come across something that I've already spent hours, months, or possibly years figuring out. I'm not a billionaire because I haven't made a billion dollars yet. I'm not a millionaire. I haven't made a million dollars, yet either. So, I have no right to teach you how to make a million dollars. I'm not famous. I'm not a rockstar. I'm not a politician or a public figure.

"So why are you writing a book, Isaac? What can you offer? What makes your way of life different to mine and how the hell could you be an inspiration to me? What are you even good at? Anything?"

These are questions I assume you may have on your mind. These are questions that I ask myself before I sit down and begin writing. As my long distance, digital mentor, Tai Lopez, would say, "What's his worth-a-damn factor?"

I would have to begin to answer this question by telling you a little bit about myself, and how my way of thinking has changed over time. I intend to be transparent and honest throughout this entire book.

I tend to compare myself with other people's lives on social media. This has become a problem because they're not transparent. They only post the best moments of their life. They want likes and recognition on the days they are (for once) doing something they enjoy. They don't do things they enjoy very often, so when they find themselves happy and in the moment they take as many pictures as they can, find the best lighting, and archive their posts for a later date for when they're feeling down and sad.

I know this because I am guilty of doing the same thing. It's gotten a little out of hand. Even on my own Instagram, Snapchat, or Facebook, you may think I have all my shit figured out. It might appear that I'm making a bajillion dollars or that I have a really successful career, but success is a matter of opinion. On the inside, before I post, I've had to change my way of thinking.

Is this a photo that will help someone? Am I posting this photo just to get a couple of double taps? Am I posting this photo to promote something? Am I honest or am I embellishing a little too much? What's the point?

I don't want to be a liar. I have no intention of fooling you or making you believe that I have it all figured out (like the rest of the people we stalk when our lives aren't quite where we think they should be). What does "should be" even mean? Where *should* your life be, right now?

In all honesty, if you had a million dollars handed to you, in cash, at this very moment, you would be doing the same thing you are doing right now: reading this book. You are here for a reason. Through all the choices you have made up until this point in your life, you are here because you chose to be--whether you realize it or not--and whether you accept that or not is your choice. I am not here to convince you. You'll come around to understanding soon enough when you look back and see that you have made some wonderful choices to make your life better, or it may hit you when you see how far you've come.

Your life *IS* where it should be at this very moment. If you can wrap your head around that, I promise you, *THAT* is happiness. Full transparency, I have written the majority of this book from the basement of my youngest brother's girlfriend's mother's house. By my own choices I have landed here, and by my own choices, once this book is published, I will be somewhere else. Who knows where. That little bit of mystery excites me.

I used to think, *I want more money. I want a better paying job. I want a girlfriend. I want a nice car. I want a car that doesn't break down all the time. I want to go to the gym. I want a six-pack. I want to eat healthier. I want to be happy. I want to be in love. I want to buy a house. I want to be a good Father. I want to take care of my family. I want to work less.*

Do you notice a pattern? I want! I want! I want! It gets pretty repetitive, doesn't it? If you take a step back and kind of audit your own life, you will see some things you wish you could change. Wishes won't change a damn thing. Effort and making a single decision to try something that could, possibly, benefit you and the people around you is a risk that some people may not want to take. That's their decision. To step outside of your comfort zone for a second and try something that you have always wanted to try could be really scary. I know this because I have been taking these risks for as long as I can remember and people always say, "I don't know how you do it. I've always wanted to do that. I'm so jealous!"

It occurred to me that some people my age (27) are parents and are unable to take the same risks. However, because I am legally single and have zero dependents, I've been able to make some mind-boggling moves whenever I felt like it. Sometimes *I* even think I'm going crazy.

"What are you getting at, Isaac? I still don't know what you do or what you're good at doing. Do you have a special skill or

something? Are you a magician? Do you think you're a motivational life coach? I don't get it!"

I don't want to come across as a motivational life coach or someone yelling at you, saying you're wrong, and everything you've ever believed is backward. I only want to help you make the decision you've always had a hard time making for yourself. I can't make it for you. So, let me answer your questions:

When I was done writing the second draft of this book I contacted a few friends to have them read it, and possibly give me some guidance on where they felt I was heading, and if I got my point across. They said I was all over the place, and that I seemed to try a whole bunch of things, get bored, and quit. This was the perfect advice for me. Now, I was challenged to come up with a defensive game plan for my way of thinking. I had to figure out why I was writing this book, to begin with. It hurt. It was an information overload when I got the feedback. Honestly, I wanted to stop writing this book and give up altogether. That's not a joke. Part of me said, "Fuck you," to the people that were helping me. Part of me said, "Thank you so much for lending a hand." I was caught between the opinions of others and my own thoughts. I had to take a week or two off from writing.

I spent those weeks thinking, *What am I good at? Do I have a special skill? What gives me the right to publish a book? Why should anyone read this? Why would they listen? Who am I? Why am I doing this? Why did I write over three hundred pages in the second draft if I had nothing to say? What's the underlying message that would benefit just one reader?*

Then it hit me. I kept thinking about my conversation with my good friend, Luke Younger, when he told me, "Isaac, what I find interesting about you, is that I could drop you anywhere and I know you'd figure it out. What do listeners of your podcast say? What's their feedback?"

"I don't know," I said, "I guess that they love my energy and optimism."

"There you go! That's it. Your enthusiasm for life and learning is what attracts people to you. You don't even have to try. I like hanging out with you because you're always up to something new. Something that you're passionate about and even if it's not working like you thought it would, you're still positive."

His words combined with a conversation I had with another friend of mine, who is an accountant, locked everything into place and made me rewrite the opening to this book.

When I was talking to my math friend he said, "Isaac, you need to perfect one skill. You aren't making a lot of money, but you could be. I think you spread yourself too thin and haven't perfected one craft. Every time I talk to you, you're doing something different. You have one skill that comes naturally to you, and that is the one that you should make money from. Like me, I'm good at math."

He was all about money, so I replied, "Being an expert at something and having one title sounds extremely boring to me. I hate being labeled as a woodworker, a carpenter, a videographer, a photographer, a gym rat, a rapper, a producer, an artist, an actor, a model, a podcast host, a motivational speaker, or anything else that boxes me into one career path."

"I get it, bro, but you need to make money!"

A little aggressive and right at his throat, I shot back with, "Dude, listen, if I wanted to be an accountant I would go to

Youtube right now, I'd find as much as I could for free, maybe pay for a course, or two, then *I* would be able to do what *you* paid for a college degree to do in less than a year. I promise you, if I want to learn something I do whatever it takes, dive right in, and learn as much as I can until I'm able to charge someone for that service or knowledge. I guess you would be paying me because I would be considered an 'expert' in that field. Even the word 'expert' pisses me off. Every time I think that someone is an expert, I am sadly disappointed when I find out that what they knew or what made them an expert, I knew already or could have Googled."

"Alright, Isaac. I bet you could do that. It's not that hard. I just think you are so talented and should be making top dollar for talents people don't even know you have yet."

I felt bad. He was just trying to help. I didn't mean to jab him like that but *I* was so confused about *why* I was doing what I was doing, and why his advice offended me so much. I couldn't see what he was saying. I couldn't understand why he would want to sit at a desk all day and do one thing for the rest of his life. It sounded horrific to me.

There were a few other people there that night and one of them told me, "I just quit my job. I feel a bit lost without the security of a job and consistent income."

I stopped. I knew that feeling all too well and I actually enjoy that feeling quite a bit.

"What do you enjoy doing?" I asked.

"Well, I want to do a podcast. A buddy and I created an LLC, opened a bank account, came up with twenty episodes of a podcast, and I don't know...we're just procrastinating."

"So, what's the next step? Do you have a microphone? What

else do you need to start?" I asked that because I may have been able to help. I had just recorded podcast episode "#TPID107" earlier that day (with Richard Nwaoko) in my car. That's where I've recorded most of my podcast episodes, and I have all the sound equipment.

"Well, we went to the guitar place...ah...you know, that..."

He didn't sound enthusiastic about the project at all. I could hear it. He sounded defeated before he even started. "Guitar Center!" I offered.

"Yeah, that's the one. I don't know, we just never bought the mic."

Having recorded over one hundred episodes of, *That Podcast With Isaac Danna*, struggling to set it up, and finding the motivation to continue, I tried to inspire him. "You don't need a mic, bro. You can use your phone, and I can help host it for a little while. I know a few fantastic podcasts that are just recorded on an iPhone. Just start! That's the important part."

He just kept coming up with excuses, and they sounded very similar to thoughts that cross my mind often. When those thoughts cross my mind I just do something about it, and don't wait. Sometimes I think I'm procrastinating, but yet I still find myself making very tough decisions extremely quickly, and not looking back.

I thought, *Is this my special skill that comes so effortlessly? Is this what makes me want to learn and try new things often? Is this what people gravitated towards? Is this what makes me want to help so many people?* Coming to find out, yes. Yes, it is.

After weeks of looking inward and trying to articulate and defend my beliefs, I finally realized what I was trying to defend. If you want to use the word expert, I guess you could say I am an 'expert' at being myself. I have no desire to be anyone else.

"Oh, that sounds a little too easy, Isaac. Can you do anything else?"

Not really! It's actually not as easy as you'd think. Let's go back to social media. When I go to post a video promoting my podcast or another product that I created or helped create, I want to get dressed in better clothes, get a haircut, and travel to a location that would inspire others. Going LIVE from the basement with a boiler and a furnace behind me that are constantly rumbling over my voice doesn't look or sound attractive. There are still people I know that think it's hilarious, and that I am worse off than them because I'm in a basement. Should I fake it all?

It would be a complete farce on my end because I practically live in this basement and rarely leave because I have designed it to be cozy and inspiring. I do all my work from this little palace made up of copper pipes, pine joists, a cement floor, two walls of sheetrock, and two walls of cinder blocks. I've got a love seat in here, a TV, my desk, iMac, Xbox One, and a ton of books. Why should I be embarrassed? I don't wear a suit every day; I wear hoodies and tee shirts, I wear the same three pair of pants until they have holes in them, I wear the same sneakers for everything, and I've even hosted premieres in bright neon Asics before.

I get a weird feeling when I try to impress someone else. I feel as if I have to stop being myself and it makes me very uncomfortable. Who cares? I can't begin to explain how happy I am, and it's all because of my particular skill, summed up in a few words:

I am an expert at being myself, and I have a passion for learning and inspiring others to learn.

Honestly, I have to tell you this so you don't just see the best bits when this gets published. I started writing this book as someone who wanted to be an "Author" rather than just writing and allowing the title of "Author" to be given to me by default after publishing the book. I started with a few short stories about my life and who I am--which are pretty entertaining--but don't have any meaning or substance except for being written and published so that I could call myself an "Author." I wrote about sixty pages and stopped. For a year. Something was missing.

I want to remove these chapters and short stories so badly and only show you the part of the book that flows seamlessly, but that would go against everything I am trying to say. I want you to see my mistakes, I want you to see that it's easier than you think, I want you to want to write a book and use your own stories (that will most likely be better than mine) and publish it. It doesn't matter the length. Just do it. My goal is to help you realize it's never too late to start something, and you can try anything you want. Don't be afraid to fail.

With that being said, the book starts off with some fun little stories that introduce you to who I am: A little bit about growing up, a bit about why I was chasing money for a while, and how it has affected me. There is a little bit about how investing in myself is the best thing I can do and how you can do it, too. Again, I am not a millionaire yet, but I do know how to survive outside of The Rat Race. I know how to work for myself and only answer to me, and I know how to do whatever I want, whenever I want. I know how to be happy, I know how to control how much negativity I allow to be around me, I know how to make someone smile and laugh, and so much more. I hope this book sparks a little something inside of you.

Again, you are going to see the rough edges of the book. Some chapters are extremely short, and some chapters are incredibly long. It goes to show you that if you don't know *why* you are doing something, you will feel lost and unfulfilled until you find your "*why*." Watch the book change as soon as I find out who I am writing to, and how I can help them.

It will be edited and rearranged a little bit. Hopefully, to make more sense for you as the reader. This is currently the eighth draft, and I have come back and edited this part to show you how many drafts it took to complete this book. I don't know of another book doing that. I thought it could be helpful to have some sort of idea how much work you can expect to put in if you decide to write your own book one day. Which, I hope you do!

Enjoy! :)
    Isaac Danna

1

THE ORIGINAL INTRODUCTION

Walking into a library is one of my favorite things to do. I guess it's just because they're so peaceful and silent, and silence is one of the many things in life that we don't experience enough of. In my opinion, taking a moment and sitting in a place with little to no noise, is rather hard to come by these days. Notifications and banners seem to alert me, and interrupt my train of thought--no matter how slightly--once a minute. I'm not even that popular...yet! I can't imagine what it will be like in the near future. Maybe, I'll create an app, allowing only the most important notifications to get through and show up on my phone. Who knows? Maybe, it already exists. If it does, you're holding out on me, man. Where can I download something like this? Will I need to scroll all the way to the last home screen just to drag it all the way back to the first home screen? I really don't have time for that. What apps could I afford to remove or reorganize to create space for it? I have them all laid out so perfectly. It really has become a science for productivity and convenience, hasn't it? Is it just me?

As my fingers fumble across the keys of my MacBook Pro, I flip my phone over, put it off to the side, and try to forget that my life revolves around this tiny, beautifully designed, masterpiece of a satellite communicator. Guess what? That still doesn't increase my focus. A notification pops up on my computer informing me that my film scanner needs an update.

Out of all things, why now? Why is it ready, right this very second, for an update? Was I about to log in and scan something? No! Was I about to start writing a biography? Yes!

Anyways, back to what I was saying: I sit down and began to type. To my left, a beautiful little girl with blonde curls races up to the windows running along the entire length of the back of the library.

The building is perched on a hill just high enough to overlook baseball fields that are so much better kept now than when I used to play ball--which, by the way, I'm very happy to see. I remember the infield having green grass where sand should have been, and chalk lines? What the hell were chalk lines?

Foul? Aw, come on! That looked fair to me, ump!

I watch the sprinting little girl sit on the ledge by the window, as she creates her own seat--her mother was behind me, and clearly used to this sort of thing--and after making herself comfortable, the little girl says to herself, *"This is what I always wanted. This is perfect."*

I swear I wasn't supposed to hear that, but she was so passionate about the view and everything around her. She had a wonderful moment to herself, and I was there witnessing it. Her face was radiating with happiness and joy. Did I also feel the same way about the environment in which I found myself? Now that I think about it, yes, I did. I just forgot how to express what I was truly feeling, because to "adult" means you have to bury any sort of emotion that surfaces immediately, as to not scare the people around you. When was the last time you saw a grown man talk to himself under his breath and exude happiness? Never. However, I can think of plenty of other things that I've heard from a grown man's mouth when speaking under his breath, and you may hear one or two of those phrases later on in this book.

This book is going to be a mixture of thoughts, ideas, experiments, and experiences I've been fortunate enough to remember thus far. I wanted to jot it all down before I got too old to remember some of the best and worst moments of my life, so consider yourself used. I am using you, the reader, as my way of letting my brain relax. I swear I feel crazy. First off, what does crazy actually mean? Well, I'm glad you asked. If you look it up, the word "crazy" means mentally deranged, especially as manifested in a wild or aggressive way. However, it also means extremely enthusiastic. To be honest, I think it's safe to say the word fits because I have so many things to talk about — so many things to say.

I don't care if you don't agree, and I don't care if you do agree. Judgment is something I am willing to face, and it wouldn't be the first time. You try writing a book! See if you have the balls to take everything you can possibly think of and write it down. I'll be the first to admit that this shit is hard. It's taken me months of saying, "I'm going to write a book. I'm writing a book. I am writing a book. What's that? No! Yea! I'm...writing a book!"

Also, until February of 2016, I never fully believed that my life was good enough or different enough for someone to be interested. For your own sake, please read this with a grain of salt: the way I think is not so usual. I ask questions, and I have a lot of what some people call "common sense," have you heard of it? I'm here to tell you that common sense is not so common. In fact, there's an overwhelming amount of people that don't make any sense at all.

2

BROTHERLY LOVE

When I was younger, I was always outside doing something. I was cutting grass, weed whacking, moving wood, helping my dad fix a car, and shooting my siblings with our incredibly dangerous hockey stick rifles--I'll tell you what, those things are deadly, man. My brother, Pete, actually killed a chipmunk with it one time. He would tell you the story better than I can, but I just remember him nailing this thing while it was running. I'm pretty sure that's the only time in the history of mankind that a Fisher Price product was used as a murder weapon. We didn't know any better though, and moving targets were just another challenge. Mission accomplished. I feel like an accomplice now, not going to lie. Poor Pete, I used to get him into trouble all of the time for no reason and I can't even remember why.

However, I remember this one time, we had just gotten back from one of those drag races in New Hampshire. They had funny cars and dragsters, you know, all kinds of stuff. I remember Dad had bought both of us little replicas of one of the dragsters. Of course, Pete and I were playing and racing them in the hallway as soon as we got home. Obviously, we wanted to prove who's car was better even though they were the exact same toy in different colors. We decided to roll them on the floor in the hall and see who's car made it to the other side of the hallway the fastest. I lost.

I was so outraged I proceeded to play by myself with *my* car and crashed it into the side of the Racetrack...otherwise known as the wall. Of course, it broke. It didn't smash into little pieces but I definitely remember the front of the dragster was missing a wheel or two. When Dad arrived, I blamed Pete for breaking something that my Father had just purchased with his hard earned money, just to watch Pete get in trouble. He still hates me for that, ask him.

Another time we were outside playing basketball together. My driveway was just off of the street, and it wasn't the kind of driveway where you have to take a mini vacation and book transportation just to get to the mailbox. I always wanted one of those *super* long driveways, though. You know, the ones that have a gate when you enter through the front? However, mine was more along the lines of something you might see driving down a country road. Specifically, the random dirt areas for emergency stops on the side of the road. The kind that the cops always back into and turn their lights off, while they wait for drivers with lead feet to fly by. Literally, the only difference may have been that mine was paved.

It wasn't a super small driveway but it was smaller than half a basketball court. So, half-court shots were taken from the road and sometimes the other side of the street. Mind you, this is a main road and cars would fly down this road at around 50-60mph. My Dad used to park the car at the entrance of the driveway just in case the ball would bounce off the backboard extra hard and get away from us. Clever move, I gotta give it to him.

There were no painted lines on our basketball court, and any side-walk chalk washed away within minutes of it raining, so we would have to guess and estimate whether or not the shots were worth two or three points when somebody scored. Usually, that meant it would depend on whether you shot behind the leaf or the pebble, though obviously these weren't laid out by us. We would just look at the ground and say, "Pebble. Leaf. Three points!"

The same scoring method was used when we would play wiffle ball. A leaf or a rock was home plate and sometimes we'd change it up with a branch or something.

Pete and I were playing a game and we got pretty competitive--you may see where this is going. I lost, yet again. Being such a sore loser, I walked over to Pete and shoved him. I don't specifically recall the action that led to Pete rolling around on the ground in the fetal position, but what I do remember was towering over him while he was down on the ground and kicking him square in the tailbone.

He squirmed, begging and yelling, "STOP! Aaaaah! What is wrong with you?"

One kick, even though I should have never assaulted him, was all I needed to even the score. To this day, I still don't remember how I never got in trouble for that. I was always trying to hurt him or get him in trouble. He was such a pain in my ass all the time. All he had to do was look at me wrong, and since I'm his older brother I wouldn't tolerate it for a second. I would immediately start talking shit, and if the argument wasn't going my way the only thing I had to do was raise my voice.

I'd yell, "PETE!"

We'd hear, "PETE, leave Isaac alone!"

Even if my Mother was a mile away in the house, it was like a reflex reaction. Every time, guilty until proven innocent.

"Na Na, Na NA," Sticking my tongue out at him.

"But Mom, I didn't even do anything!" he'd wail, but it didn't matter.

Somehow he was always in trouble, and since he was always in trouble, it just became easier and easier to get him into more shit. In fairness, a lot of the times I didn't even know what he was in trouble *for*. Dad used to get pissed off rather easily about absolutely nothing and everything at the same time.

I'm one of four children in the Danna family. I also happen to be the oldest. My siblings and I are all two years apart from each other. Fun fact number one is that we were all homeschooled for a period of time. (Oh, yeah, there's more to that story, don't worry.) Fun fact number two is that if our ages were odd numbers, our grade numbers were even. If our ages were even numbers, our grade numbers were odd. I don't know why, but I always found that so amusing.

Unfortunately, when we were forced to go to public school, three of us could never end up in the same school at the same time because of our age differences. The maximum amount of Danna children would only be two. If one person was moving up and entering a new school, one of us would be on our way out. We used to joke around and say that one of us should stay back just to hang out. The funny thing was that it would have had been myself or Pete since he was two years younger than I was, and neither of us thought that was a good idea. However, we did seriously consider it just so we would be able to have a crew and our classmates would be like, "Don't fuck with the Danna's." We really wanted to create a little family gang.

This reminds me if we somehow became skilled musicians and started a band, I wanted to name the group, "Bandanna." Band-Danna, BanDanna, get it? Great Dad joke! Too bad we had zero musical talent, and we never ended up with those T-Bird jackets with patches on the back, arms, and chest. I'm still pretty sore about it if you can't tell.

I take that back, my sister Naomi has some serious vocals. Growing up, her and I would sing famous pop songs and argue over the lyrics. She has a better voice than I do, but I wrote lyrics more than she did because I attempted rapping for a while. We would argue so much about lyrics that we started keeping track of our wins and losses on the fridge. This was when Google was just becoming really popular for looking shit up. We ended up moving to another house and lost the "Game's Scoreboard" in the process. I like to say that *I* won but she definitely reminds me all the time that she was in the lead right before we "mysteriously" lost the scoreboard. I know she's telling the truth but I like to tease her.

Speaking of teasing, I used to make fun of her weight. Even when she was trying to lose it, I would say things like, "Looks like you're in a comfortable relationship..."

We all know what that means. She made sure to get me back when I gained forty-five pound after I moved to NYC, though.

She saw me one day and said, "Isaac, *you* look like *you're* in a comfortable relationship!"

That dug deep.

The same day, my Grandfather tapped my newly acquired stomach and said, "You're looking like you put on some weight there, kid!"

After that day, I realized how horrible it was to make fun of her when we were younger. Naomi, if you're reading this, I hope you will forgive me. I never meant to hurt you!

You know who's feelings don't get hurt much? Joe's! My youngest brother, of six years, has been an inspiration to me. When he decides to do something, he focuses and accomplishes that goal. He wanted to be a Marine so he signed up, went through hell, and became a United States Marine. Then, he wanted to become a Firefighter--like my father and grandfather--so he signed up, studied, did whatever it took to pay for the classes, and got it done!

Meanwhile, I'm over here like, "Hi...I'm just an artist trying to live my life and learn as much as I can."

Sometimes I am so jealous of how successful he has been but then I realize that he looks at me the same way. He's even told me that he's proud of me for focusing on my dreams, taking action, never giving up, and making them a reality. As of recent years, I'm proud to say that we've actually strengthened our relationship because I ended up moving in with him after he offered to help me chase my dream by giving me a cheap room.

In turn, I hired him to work with me for a little while. Well, until I realized that I had been basically paying for his vacation time. We would just laugh and do fun things instead of actually being productive, so when I ran out of money, he understood. That being said, while he was working with me he created an entire book club designed around affiliate links and helped me get my first one hundred subscribers. Joe and Pete, even helped me produce some short films.

Notes To The Fam:

I want to thank each and every one of you for helping me fully focus on being myself. It doesn't matter what I learn or do, you make me feel like I am successful and doing the right thing. Even if you don't understand what the hell I'm talking about, you still act like it's the biggest thing since sliced bread and I appreciate that. I know I bounce around from thing to thing but it's all because I'm in love with knowledge and helping others.

3

SNEAKY REVIEWS

Going to the movies is still my favorite thing to do. To be honest, I got into online marketing, sales, and automated income because I wanted to learn how to sell movies and create production companies. There is magic in the cinema. Goosebumps still randomly appear every time I go to the cinema, and I do mean randomly. In fact, I get the chills as soon as I feel the rumbling of the bass from a theatre while I am in the hall searching for my theatre. Maybe it's the air conditioning...Just kidding! There's just something about arriving before the previews, sitting down, and getting a good seat. Most people hate previews or arrive late. I get really upset if I don't time the movie right because I think your ticket pays for the preview too. Think about it, they're little mini-movies.

I also enjoy watching people walk in and try to find eight seats in a row, for their entire wedding party, it's hilarious.

I think, *Come on, Bro! When you arrive during the previews and walk in with twenty people, don't get mad when you can't find three seats in a row. Let alone eight.*

They're like, "What the fuck? I knew we should have taken Jefferson to get here."

"Dude, if you didn't drive like your dead grandmother, we wouldn't have had to park four lots away. That's what it was, it wasn't the route."

Meanwhile, I'm sitting there like, *Yeah, that's it. It's the way he drives. It's definitely not the fact that you don't know how to coordinate with seven friends and have no common sense.*

Learn how to organize an event and get there early, it's that simple. You could also do what I do and go alone. You will always find a seat. Actually, I have a confession to make: You won't be able to do this if the owner of AMC reads this book, but in Manhattan, my ex and I found a movie theatre that had multiple floors. Being from a small town and all, a multi-level movie theatre fucking blew my mind. We would use Google or the Moviefone app to check out movie times and add up the total length of the times and see which movies lined up. Usually, we'd watch the one we were most interested in first. Then, we would leave the theatre after the movie was done, hoping there was no secret video message in the credits. (We would try to leave after respecting the cast and crew, obviously, because so much work is put into making movies. How could you not appreciate the names at the end?) Before we watched the first movie, we would walk around and try to get an idea of where we would have to run after the first movie ended since we didn't want to miss the previews of the second movie we wanted to watch.

Sometimes it would work, but sometimes the first movie was on the first floor and we would have to travel all the way up to the fourth floor for our second flick. The only catch was, the theatre started catching on so they hired someone to man the elevator.

Hold on, as I wrote "man", I am all for women but I personally would never in my life be able to say that phrase and replace the word "Man" with "Woman". They hired someone to "Woman" the elevator. I'm literally laughing out loud as I write this. Not because I don't think a woman should be checking tickets or be in control of who enters and exits the elevator, but because the phrase sounds so outdated in 2017. With women being so powerful and making serious movies, that whole phrase seems ridiculous and obviously dates back to the old days when women were expected to be housewives. I guess they would have "Womaned" the house just fine and that wasn't even a question? I don't know. It's fucked up.

I did it again, you have to keep me on track here people. Jesus! Okay, so there was this one time we started on the *first floor*. That's where our first movie was on that day. The ideal plan would have been to watch our first movie all the way up on the fourth floor, not the first floor, and work our way down slowly, walking around on each floor to see where the second movie was playing. As we entered the elevator, there was a young man (or should I say boy) that was obviously new to this whole thing. You could tell he cared but had zero authority.

"What floor?"

There were more than a few people crammed in that elevator and I remember we all said in sync, "Four, please."

The boy proceeded to check everyone's tickets. Everyone else, suspended in this little death chamber on cables, passed this test with flying colors. Naturally, they were attending their *first* movie. As we completely ignored him looking directly at us, he asked, "May I see your tickets?"

He asked at least three times to see them. We just kept staring at the numbers lit up on the wall as they kept increasing. It was the most awkward sixty seconds of my life. Well, at the time anyway. There are plenty of awkward "Sixty Second" stories that I may or may not mention in the future, that I can assure you.

Everyone in the elevator looked at us and couldn't believe we just defied the rules of the cinema. "Oh My God!" I could see their faces in my peripherals.

The door opened and we just walked out as if we were deaf and never heard a thing. First of all, don't judge! Second, I will own a fucking movie theatre one day and let people watch movies for FREE...sometimes. I am sure karma will come back around because it's kind of like robbery, but listen, if you don't have a system in place that prevents this sort of thing, then it will keep happening. They obviously don't care too much because it is way more money to pay someone $10/hr to sit there for 8 hours. In fact, most of the movies you watch have at least one or two seats open anyways. It is extremely rare to walk into a completely packed theatre.

Therefore, I truly believe that I am one more set of eyes to watch someone's hard work. I also truly believe that *I* should be the one getting paid to go watch these movies because I promote movies so much to people. I'll often say, "Have you seen this?

Have you seen that? Aw, you gotta watch this one! You haven't seen that yet? Why? What is wrong with you?"

So, therefore, I have come to conclude that a free movie ticket would cost a lot less than paying someone to tell a certain number of people how good the movie was. By sneaking into these movies, I could potentially save *YOU* money by telling you it was shitty and not to waste your money. So, you're welcome. Don't mention it.

I gotchu boo. You could save 15% or more by switching to Sneakyreviews.com.

Again, you're welcome. This could be your next business opportunity. Congrats on your future endeavors.

Where was I? Oh, yes. Once upon a time my ex and I went to a matinée for $6. We watched one movie and then went to see another. Then another. I will say that $2 per movie is an amazing deal, am I wrong? How can you get mad at that? I used my brain power to study and learn from the magic that is cinema.

I truly enjoy the movies more than anything, and I am fortunate enough to have worked on a few projects myself. The last movie I worked on was called *Yellow Scare*. It was my very first feature film, and "audio recordist" was my IMDB title, I believe. It was quite the experience and I met a lot of wonderful people.

After that, I worked on what is going to be a massive hit in the online world. It's a web-series/TV show about an African-American gentleman searching for independence, and the struggles of becoming a man. Written, directed, and starring Richard Nwaoko. Maybe you'll have heard of this guy by the time you read this book. He's one of my best friends and just so happens to be an extremely talented individual. I had the pleasure of producing the pilot episode using my equipment and production skills. I'm the cinematographer, video editor, audio engineer, and I even act in it as well. It's an ongoing production so these credits will vary per episode or season, but keep an eye out for *Becoming*. How do you like that little sales pitch for another product?

As I write this, there is a new app out that actually charges you $9.99/month and you can watch one movie per calendar day at the cinema. Seriously! That's not a joke. We'll see how long that lasts. I've been using MoviePass for a couple of months now and I love it. Too bad I don't get paid for these referrals, huh? Apparently, that's just how much I believe in these products.

4

TOO COOL FOR SCHOOL

My first day of public school was when I was entering the fifth grade. Here is how the story goes, though my dad will tell you otherwise, you can decide who you think is telling the truth.

My neighbor was in eighth grade and she used to babysit us for time to time. She lived just across the street so it was perfect for my parents. I was three years younger than she was, but that didn't matter to me at all. I had a crush on her. Relax, nothing ever happened. Get your mind out of the gutter, you sicko. Between you and me, I wanted something to happen so badly but I was homeschooled so I had no clue what "something" even was at the time. I just knew that she was really nice and sweet

She used to let me go to bed right as my parents were pulling in the driveway. She also taught me a trick for completely convincing my parents that I had been in bed for hours and was sound asleep. See, the bed needed to be warm as if I was lying there for hours and was a good son. (Again, get the mind out of the damn gutter. Jesus!) Okay, so the technique was as follows: Since I was going to bed right when they pulled in the driveway, I had to work quickly. What she recommended I do, was to jump in bed and essentially act as if I was having a fit or a spasm. Then the blankets would go all over the place, the pillows would move, and the sheets would untuck themselves. This was to represent hours of movement.

Wait, that's not all, there's more. If you order right now....No, I won't. I'll spare you. She told me that if I laid there and sprawled out like I was making snow angels, then moved my arms and legs back and forth at a ridiculously rapid pace, the sheets would start to warm up. I was told to keep doing that until they walked into the room to check on me. Even if they sat on the edge of the bed to kiss me goodnight, guess what? They'd fall for it. Everything would be warm and cuddly as if I was sleeping like a baby.

Looking back, the only thing she miscalculated was the increased heart rate. That being said, I never got caught. They would come into my room and I would hear their footsteps. It was never both of them, it was always just one. I could tell if it was my mom or my dad by the sound of the shoes. I mean, if you want to call me "Sherlock" that's fine, but the sound of heels was probably not my father, right? Right! So it was a fifty-fifty chance, and my odds were pretty good.

Although, one time I heard heels and the next thing I know my dad's scruffy beard sanded away my forehead as he kissed me goodnight. My only guess would be that he was carrying my mom's heels for her as she went to their room, and then he decided to bend over and start placing the heels on the floor while walking them with his hands to my room......I totally made all that up. That never happened, I swear. How funny would it be though? Dads are clever. If you give any sign of you being clever at a young age, they know the game.

In all seriousness, the whole sanding my forehead thing happened all the time. I swear he just taped 60 grit sandpaper to his chin and purposefully tried to refinish my face. Maybe it's the caveman way to exfoliate? That must be what it was. Sorry, I did it again.

Anyways, I never got caught. My baby sitter was like a sexy magician. Usually, it was my mom who would come in and sit on the side of the bed to say goodnight and tuck me in...tuck me in. I must have been moving too much while I was asleep. Clearly, it worked. This nameless neighbor was lovely. We'll get back to her.

The morning of my first day of fifth grade was horrendous. I was wearing some sort of vest from Walmart along with Faded Glory jeans. If you don't know what Faded Glory jeans are, I am so, so, so happy for you.

My dad was cooking us all breakfast and he was making egg sandwiches. The egg sandwich was what I was supposed to eat right before this life-changing day. He took the eggs and gently placed them on an English Muffin (I love those by the way, though I used to love them more before this event) before handing me the sandwich. Dad's cooking is about ninety percent delicious every time.

I took a bite thinking, *Oh, why not? I've had one before.*

My mouth immediately told me that something wasn't tasting right. I looked at the bottom of the sandwich and it was black. He burnt the shit out the only good thing in my life at that moment. So, now my life just sucks entirely. In my house, you cannot let food go to waste so I forced myself to eat charcoal and eggs for breakfast but let me tell you, that did not cure the butterfly conservatory that was my stomach.

Not only was I going to be thrown to the wolves in less than twenty minutes, but my sexy neighbor offered to sit with me on the bus. This was a big deal. I was going to be on a bus full of people and faces that I had never seen in my life, and my social skills included killing chipmunks with Fisher Price hockey sticks and kicking tail bones. You can imagine how nervous I was. Plus, I still had a crush on her.

This big yellow rocket to hell arrived at my basketball court and opened its doors to welcome me. As I stepped up onto the bus, I remember nothing from that moment except seeing my neighbor, who was gesturing for me to sit with her. She slid in and I remember having a moment of relaxation. No more than just a moment. As the bus began to move, the butterfly conservatory began to rumble again. "Flutter" is too beautiful of a word to use here, because what my stomach was going through was far from beautiful. I *could* just make this whole thing up and pretend to explain the entire bus ride, but I don't actually remember any of it.

No, that's a lie. The last thing I remember is looking up as my neighbor said, "Are you okay? Isaac!" My face must have been noticeably pale in that moment.

I turned to my right and faced the aisle, kind of, just as the butterflies broke out of the conservatory and flew all over the front of me, the seat in front of me. Meanwhile, I still have a crush on the young lady next to me. That feeling never really went away except that now, in addition to my attraction, embarrassment was all over my cheeks...and probably my chin too. I genuinely cannot tell you what happened next. I don't even remember cleaning it up or anyone else helping clean it up for that matter.

We arrived at my new middle school, and one by one we all avoided the butterflies in the aisle and stepped off the bus, ready to take on part two. What could possibly be worse than throwing up in front of what could have been a bus full of potential friends, and the one girl that you wanted to impress with Faded Glory jeans and a sweater vest?

I'll tell you, the day is a blur for good reasons. I never really wanted to relive that day but unfortunately, I experienced another episode hours later. Bells were ringing and people were running around like crazy people to this open area where everyone was racing to get in line. At the front of the line there appeared to be trays being given to students with food on them. I can't remember if my parents had packed lunch for me or if I tried to get in line but this *whole thing* was new to me. I was used to sitting with my brothers and sister around a dinner table and eating sandwiches, fish sticks, or imitation lobster.

Yum. Oh, how I miss those days.

I remember attempting to sit at a table and make friends or something. I also remember trying to eat, but again I do not recall if it was of my parent's creation or the school's. I attempted to eat and immediately ran to the front of what they call a cafeteria, to seek out the largest trash bin I could find. Of course, the trash just so happened to be in plain sight of the entire cafeteria. Did I mention that by standing up while everyone else was seated, I was already the center of attention? Running to the bin didn't lessen the attraction from the eyes of my peers. I leaned into the big gray bucket that could have consumed my entire body if I bent over low enough, and believe me, I tried to bury my face as deep as I could in that trash bin, but round two of the butterflies decided to fly out and destroy yet another moment of my childhood.

Next thing I knew, I was in the nurse's office where I had to stay until my mother came to pick me up. Guess what class I missed? I made sure to attend all the boring classes and welcoming homerooms, but I had to skip computer class. They wouldn't let me go back to classes, thank God, but even so, I find it rather ironic that now I am so into technology, computers, e-commerce and anything online related. Maybe all that happened for a reason, who knows?

So to this day, I still blame my Dad's charcoal and eggs on my misfortune. Obviously, you already know who's story to believe, mine. It had nothing to with the fact that I had no social skills and was being thrown into an environment of judgment and criticism, wearing a fucking sweater vest and Faded Glory jeans. It also had nothing to do with the fact that I didn't know how to interact with humans or how to make friends.

I swear! It was that Goddamn sandwich! Thanks, Dad!

The middle school in Charlton, Massachusetts includes grades five through eight, so elementary school is what I completely missed out on. I spent my elementary days at home cheating on tests if my mother accidentally left the Teacher's Guide on the table. I swear this only happened once, but I did so well on the test that she caught me.

Idiot!

At least make sure if you cheat to make it seem like you didn't know a few answers, right? Wrong. I copied everything, word for word and nailed every answer. Of course, when she was grading the test, she knew something was off.

"Yeah, okay, Isaac. You're not that awesome!" Those are the words I imagine she blurted out while grading. Probably with a little loving chuckle.

Moms are just great for picking up on things, aren't they? My elementary days were filled with a few hours of learning and hard work, and then playing outside in the back yard with my siblings. It wasn't all that bad. It's funny how my life is pretty much the same now. I learn and work hard from the comfort of my own home. To be honest, I had no idea what I was missing out on until I attended middle school for fifth grade. Want to know something funny? I am sure there are some other reasons but I like to tell the story this way:

My mother received her instructions for the fifth-grade curriculum stating what was "mandatory" to teach her students. One of the subjects on the list was a foreign language. Now, the only language my mother knows is English. She knows it very well too, I must say. She reads so much that my buddy, Ryan, knighted her with the nickname, "Reada," when we were growing up. I know what you're thinking, *"Isaac had friends when he was home-schooled?"*

No! Even though my mother says I had dozens of friends, I don't know where they are now. Ryan was a middle school friend.

Anyways, I'm sure my mom thought about learning another language just to teach us because that is who she is. She takes care of the family and does whatever it takes. In fairness to her, learning a new language seems like an overwhelming task to take on. Then having to teach it to four kids? Forget it! So my mom and dad decided, "That's it! Time to go to public school."

I'm sure there were more reasons than that, but that's enough for me to understand why *I* ended up having to try and stomach a burnt egg sandwich.

5

MEMORABLE MOMENTS

When I was in class one day in fifth grade, I was sitting next to this fine young fellow named Ryan. He seemed like he knew a few people and he was very nice. (This story is still one of my favorites to tell. He and I are still great friends to this day and still have the same amount of laughter about this story whenever it comes up.) Since I didn't know what people skills were, or how to socialize, or what friends were, or how to become friends, I just went for the gold. I turned to this kid, leaned in and said, "Hi!"

With subtext defined as *Fuck off*, he replied, "Hi."

I blurted out, "Will you be my friend?"

Who does this? Where did I learn that this was okay to try and do? How does one ask someone to be there friend anyway? Have you ever thought about it? It just kind of happens right? Sometimes it happens and you never even wanted to be friends with that person in the first place. You know what he said without even thinking about what I just said?

He said, "I'll get back to you."

Which is literally the best answer for that question, and I am dying of laughter as I write this. He didn't try and play it off like we were already friends, he didn't pretend to care, he didn't say no, he didn't say yes. Though, in my mind, that meant yes. Obviously. I don't remember how we actually became friends and Ryan doesn't either, we just know that we loved hanging out and playing baseball together.

His family is so nice and they used to take me to Old Orchard Beach in the summers. It started becoming a tradition, and it was amazing. I was, however, envious when he got to join boy scouts and I couldn't afford it. He had all kinds of stories about friends, and trips, and traveling, and all these stupid little inside jokes with his buddies. I was completely in the dark when they would talk around me at school. (Sorry, it is still a soft spot.)

In fact, the next friend that I attempted to acquire was also part of the boy scouts, and his name was Sean. Sean and Ryan were not friends, or I wasn't aware of their friendship if they were, until they both ended up in scouts together. Eventually, I set my sights on Sean, and I decided to go in for the kill. I had learned my lesson from Ryan's response and I wasn't about to let that awkward situation come about again. This time, I used a sneaky tactic to acquire my new friend. I mean, my intentions were good. I wanted as many "best friends" as I could have, who doesn't? I also just liked talking to people and I could already tell that school wasn't for me. We ended up sitting next to each other in one class and I leaned over and saw that he had a brand new box of pencils. I asked, "Could I borrow a pencil?"

"Sure. Here." He had no idea what hit him. Friends without him even knowing. It was perfect.

Again, I don't know how *we* officially became friends or when and unfortunately, Facebook wasn't around to tell us when I was in my fifth-grade science class. If it was, I was so far away from knowing what a fucking computer was, it's hilarious. Now, I can't live without my computers. That's right, computers. Multiple. Be jealous. Now that I landed on computers, I think it is a fitting time to say that he probably introduced me to what computers were more than anyone else, so I am blaming Sean for my constant need to converse with women via the web in those days. Remember AIM? AOL Instant Messenger? He was the king at acquiring girls' "AIMs" or whatever you called them. He had so many racked up, we could just sit around his computer and message these girls all night long. It was ridiculous. We would chat with them and then call them, then chat, and then call again. If we saw the girls in school, it was like nothing ever happened. It was a very weird time in my life. He even introduced me to porn. Thank you, Sean, you are truly The Man.

One night we were sitting at the computer, it was getting dark and his parents were going to be home soon. We were looking up naked photos or something and he was going through showing me what was what. I remember his parents were about to pull up the driveway (what a long ass driveway that was) and we could see the headlights, so we logged off and went to go play with toys that sixth graders would play with. Maybe video games or something?

We were playing and his father called his name as if he just wanted to have a casual conversation, "Sean, can you come here for a minute?"

He looks at me and says, "I'll be right back."

I said, "Okay."

He returned with his mother and father and they all looked at me like I was the only one in trouble. I'm thinking, *Wait, how does this work? Can you even punish me? You aren't my parents!*

They told us how they went through the history and pulled up the sites that we were just looking at. We both learned something that day-- if you are going to watch porn on a computer, erase your tracks and never tell a soul. Deny, deny, deny. That day we admitted that we were intrigued and wanted to see more. His parents were truly amazing people; I lucked out with great friends that had amazing parents who were so caring and loving while I was growing up.

Once we came clean, they said, "If you promise not to do it again and you learned from this mistake, we will not tell your parents, Isaac."

What? You won't tell my parents? Really? What do you want me to say? I'll say anything. Please! I'll do anything.

I was just a little boy that wanted to see female body parts. As a homeschooled child, I had no idea that the female body could be so stunning. So, I owned up to looking at the pornography on the computer and what happened next was the best punishment, ever.

They said, "Okay, good! I'm glad you have learned your lesson. Now, are we hungry boys? Want to go to Chuck's Steakhouse and grab some food?"

What the hell just happened? I looked at porn and my reward is a plate of expensive, succulent steak tips? Come on, really?

Maybe it's why I still enjoy it to this day. The steak, obviously.

On a more serious note, after I successfully made two friends I was confident enough to make other friends. The next one I should probably mention is Mike, and he lived just down the street from me. I say down the street, but it was like down the street and left down another street. Mike happened to be on my bus and he had a Walkman. I don't know if it was actually called a Walkman, but it was a CD player. I remember he used to play the best songs because I could hear them through his headphones a few seats away. At the time, he had some big ass, over the ear, over the head kind of headphones. I think he accidentally offered to share his seat with me one day, but I was ecstatic. Being homeschooled, I had no idea what pop music was or what "genres" were for that matter, so this became my own little private listening session.

I was listening to *his* music from *his* headphones that were attached to *his* head, and he didn't even mind when I kept nodding and bobbing my head. Though, when I kept asking what song it was or who the artist was, he got a little frustrated with me. To be honest, I don't even think we spoke to each other except for me begging him multiple times to tell me what song it was. I was totally content with hearing the tinny sound of hit music from someone else's headphones.

Mike introduced me to "Butterfly" by Crazy Town, and that was our favorite song for the longest time. When he allowed me to sit with him--which was most days now--he would bring the in-ear headphones, and we would share the left and right earpieces.

Aw, how adorable?

We must have looked like a couple that had been dating for a week. They try to be polite to each other because they can't be themselves yet, but neither one wanted to say, "Can you just use your own, please? I can't hear what the musician intended when they released the song. You are literally lowering the quality of this song by fifty percent."

Mike was the one that was being nice and I was taking advantage of *him*. Some days, he'd get on the bus after I got on first, and he'd sit in another seat. I noticed that on the days he sat in another seat, he would also be wearing his massive headphones, as if to say, "You ain't listening to my music today Muthah Fuckah!"

It really wasn't a problem. Yet, apparently, it still irks me a little bit. Somehow, I was jealous that he got to listen to his own music whenever he wanted while I hadn't been able to afford a pair of headphones, let alone a CD player to plug the headphones into. Again, to clarify, not Mike's fault. I just got annoyed if I had to sit in the seat alone and listen to ignorant people talk. It was totally okay if he didn't want to share ear wax with me.

One day, out of nowhere, Mike hopped on the bus and opened up his backpack. His face radiated with excitement. As he was sitting next to me, he pulled out this cord with one male end and two female ends. I had no idea what it was, and I can only imagine my dumbfounded expression compared to his super high energy at the same time. I was curious. Out of his Mary Poppins bag, he grabbed his "Fuck You!" headphones.

I'm left thinking, *This guy's an asshole, man.*

You should know that both of those words were not part of my vocabulary at that time.

Thank you, Mom and Dad.

. . .

I was thinking, *Seriously? You're just going to sit with me and smile, then bring out the headphones you can't share? Fine, I'll just listen to the muffled, rattles, of your pop music while I lean on your shoulder and try to recognize each song.*

Just as if he had read my mind, I see him grab the "sharable" in-ear headphones.

What is going on? Is he teasing me?

Mike grabs his CD player, which I believe had duct tape on it, and he plugs in what will later be understood as an auxiliary splitter. He continues to plug in both headphones and *voila!* That's when I realized that I could also listen to his music with him, but not *with* him, while at the same time ignoring ignorant people on the bus. One hundred percent music, almost exactly how the musician would have wanted me to hear it. Truly incredible. To this day, I still think it's a mind blower.

Mike's dad was a bit like mine, and his mother was friendly with my mother. I think they had met at a group event in town. The group was created by women, for women. Mom wasn't part of it for too long and what's even funnier, if I am not mistaken, Mike's mother wasn't either. Mike's parents were lovely, and they treated me like family. I would often crash over there on weekends like I would with Sean and Ryan. We all went to the same school but we were part of different cliques. Not that my very, very, embarrassingly white, safe, recently renovated middle school had "cliques" or gangs or anything.

After moving to New York City and traveling back to Charlton, Massachusetts, I noticed a severe lack of diversity in the area. I remember just a few kids with different skin color than I had, and I always remember wanting their skin tone. To me, it was a nice, dark, even tan--without the farmers tan. I actually have a lovely tan thanks to my mother's side of the family and their Native American background.

You've got to love that .01% that everyone wants to claim.

I tanned well, but not as good as these guys. Nowadays, I don't even know if I can say "these guys." It seems so politically incorrect, both racially and genderly. (I made that word up, genderly. You like it?)

Mike and I had some great times in Old Orchard Beach, up in Maine. Ryan and his family took me up there as well. Sometimes their family vacations would overlap and I was part of both vacations. That was amazing, really. Old Orchard Beach's abbreviation is OOB, and you see it on tourist stickers everywhere. Now you know what OOB is. OOB has a few rides and arcade games near the pier, so as kids we would head down to the pier at night and "people watch." It just so happens, to this day, "people watching" is still one of my favorite things to do. That's one of the reasons I love New York City so much. The sound of the arcade games in the distance and beautiful girls in bikinis, right near the beach, come on, who couldn't like that combo?

In addition, we would stop at Dairy Queen and have ourselves a Blizzard. (Side note, Blizzards are not good anymore. My taste buds have changed dramatically.) I used to down one of those things every night on vacation. Let's put it this way, I would rake a few extra leaves or stay to wash dishes if it meant I could afford another night by the pier with a Blizzard. Aside from us gawking at twenty-three-year-olds when we were fifteen or younger, we also enjoyed taking day trips further up into Maine, as well as bike rides along the coastline.

One of the most amusing things for me is that Ryan and I use to stare at girls and I was the only one that was always trying to say, "Hi."

Years later, Ryan opened up to me about being gay. That was a lovely moment by the way. I saw my best friend as an entirely different person, but a better person all in one moment. He was literally a new man. With purpose and passion.

Mike, however, is as straight as they come. You know the kind, swimwear models on graphic tees and Jenna Jameson posters on the back of bedroom doors. He and I would do the same thing, and try to talk to girls but get turned down all day long.

Except for this one time. The bathrooms were about a 5-minute walk away from the trailer, and outside of the bathrooms, there were two campsites only big enough for a few tents. There happened to be a couple of French girls from Canada staying at those sites. We ended up seeing them every time we went to the bathroom, and believe you me, we went as often as we could. They were so beautiful. Somehow we ran into them one evening, walking around the campground and we tried to talk to them. I say tried because they spoke, maybe, four words of English. One spoke better English than the other and of course, she happened to be the prettiest, so we both ended up pursuing her.

We were required to take a foreign language in middle school, remember? That's why my mom sent me on my way. It just so happened that the language Mike and I decided to take was none other than French, the language of *amour*. Horny little boys.

The girl that spoke a little bit of English, we will call her Nicole. That is not her name, but after reading this story you will know why I don't remember it. Nicole was talking to, let's call her, Anna. They were loving that American boys were flirting with them and they were giggling, and we were trying our best to understand them.

Why the fuck did we goof off in French class? Why?

Who knew that we would need to know *this* language to speak to girls in *America*? Nobody tells you this shit. We thought that the only time we would ever have to use French was if we visited France.

All of the sudden Mike and I looked at each other and said the same exact thing, at the same exact time, "La Plage! She said 'La Plage,' did you hear that?"

What did that mean?

Let's narrow it down: we had heard a word that we both knew. It had to be something fun or had to be something we understood because it was easy to remember...We weren't very bright kids at that time.

What was it? POOL! No! Wait! Beach! BEACH! They want to go to the beach with us!

We were so excited that we blurted out, "Nicole, La Plage, Oui!"

This translates into a couple of dumbasses saying, "Nicole, beach, yes!"

We all laughed and somehow set up a time to meet up with them in the morning, and head to the beach. It was really happening, girls were talking to us. We were going to see French girls in bikinis. There just might be a God.

The next morning, we walked to the bathrooms and picked

them up. After being polite to their mothers, they allowed us to take their young ladies to the beach at last. In Maine, the water is not warm by any means, but Mike and I were too young to care about our balls shriveling up and falling off. We just wanted to play games and get to know these foreign creatures of beauty. Obviously, a foam football was one of the most important things to bring to the beach. Luckily, Mike remembered to bring the ball and it was a good thing he did. We played with that ball as far out in that water as we could. We were throwing and jumping and dunking each other under the water, and the sun was glistening off the white caps as they turned into the most perfect body surfing waves. We would ride the waves to the shore and chase each other to the towels. It was so romantic and such an incredible day.

One of the girls drew her name in the sand and where she was from, and they made sure to write their numbers in the sand too, so we would never lose touch. They explained that residents of Quebec would travel down to Maine because it was rather close and they had a significant amount of vacation time. As she was telling us this, I remember looking around and all I could hear around me was the sound of French conversation and laughter. Everyone on the beach seemed to be from Canada that day, it was insane. The hours seemed to fly by faster than I could say, "Nicole, La Plage," and before we knew what happened, it was time to head back to the campground. Each of us had to get back for dinner, but we agreed that if we could convince our parents that we had such a blast and that we only live once, we would meet them by the bathrooms after dinner. If all went according to plan, we would then head on down to the pier and walk around with lovely French-speaking beauties holding *our* arms. People would be people watching *us* for the first time. We were so excited.

After dinner and a shower, we ran as fast as we could to the bathrooms. The girls were just finishing up and they looked stunning. Both sets of parents let us go to the pier and Mike's Dad agreed to pick us up later on, but not too late as those were the rules. Mike and I were still fighting over the *same* girl we both found most attractive and the most understandable. (I say fighting, because for some reason when two boys try their hardest to impress a girl they decide, *Who better to pick on than my opponent?* Why is that a thing? We should build each other up. If we're going to lie, lie for the better and create massive success stories for each other. We shouldn't bring each other down until the other drops out of the race. It seems backward.) Anyways, we were trying to impress the girls by showing them around and walking on the beach. We rode some rides and had the night of our lives.

That was all before the night took a turn for the better. How that was possible, I have no idea. Nicole was super spontaneous apparently, and she asked us to go swimming. Mind you, we were fully clothed--no bathing suits on or anything. Did I mention fully clothed? It was pitch black and we couldn't see a damn thing. The starlight wasn't bright enough to see anything and the moon wasn't full, so the only light we had was coming from the Ferris wheel behind us. Nicole ran into the water first and I had never been more turned on in my entire life. At the time she was wearing skin-tight jeans that appeared to be glued to her legs. The pants had one seam right down the middle of the back, and there were no pockets. NO POCKETS! That is sexy as fuck, to begin with. (Whoever created these pants is a legend in my eyes. Good for you! I wish I could kiss you.) As soon as she turned us on with her outfit, she returned from the ocean and started walking towards us. We were being a couple of babies. She had dived right in, and we were just in shock.

Our faces expressed a great deal of fear, *What would Mom and Dad say? Is it safe? Are there jellyfish? Did those sharks ever swim all the way up from Florida this year? What would happen if we just drowned and nobody found us? What if........SHUT THE FUCK UP AND LIVE A LITTLE BIT!*

Finally, we ran into the water and it was so exhilarating, I really can't explain the feeling. So much fear in and around every inch of my being, and there I was fully immersed in salt water next to someone who was the most beautiful young lady I had ever met...and she had an accent. Just imagine, it was against all the rules. The rent-a-cops would have kicked us off the beach if they had caught us, Mike's Dad would never let us do this, my parents would have grounded me for months, yet here I am, not a care in the world about who I will need to explain myself to, or how I am going to explain this when the time comes. It was right around this time that we were all so happy and high on life that we decided to start heading back to the amusements just off the beach; soaking wet and dripping head to toe.

As we walked back to the park, Nicole and I ended up falling behind for a second...you can see where this is going. Let me tell you, that kiss was incredible. Now, I'm in double trouble: kissing strangers *and* diving into the ocean when it's pitch black? We admired each other and embraced that irreplaceable moment.

After we caught up with the others just a few seconds later, I was smiling ear to ear. Mike was laughing but you could tell he was kind of pissed. He seemed to know what happened without me having to say a damn thing. Obviously, it was written all over my face. I told him anyway. "Bro, she just kissed me. She just kissed me."

Mike said, "That's awesome, dude. She's a good kisser, right?"

My heart stopped. "What do you mean she's a good kisser? How the *fuck* do you know?"

With absolutely no chill, he goes, "Yeah, she kissed me earlier, behind one of the rides."

I should just end the chapter here but there is more. To this day, I wholeheartedly want to believe my own friend is simply lying through his fuckin' teeth. I found holes in his story which lead me to believe it was impulsive jealousy, so hear me out:

In theory, being boys and all, *IF* Nicole, actually did kiss him earlier in the evening why didn't he tell me? Wouldn't that be the best thing since sliced bread at fourteen years old? Did he think I was going to get mad? Maybe, but that still doesn't add up. As I said earlier, we would bash each other hard just to compete for the attention of every girl we would talk to. This is a fact. So, again, *IF* this did happen, why wouldn't he have just rubbed it in my face before I continued trying? Or, did he just take it one step further with the jabbing and wait for the perfect time to throw the right hook? Either way, he got me good. My night was totally ruined. To top it off, his father was on his way to pick us up and we weren't sure if we were ever going to see these Frenchies again. Talk about distraught.

I hopped up into the backseat of the cab, in his father's pick up truck. I don't remember if we called ahead and had him bring us towels, I just remember part of me dying inside and part of me being so full of life that I didn't know what to do while I was sitting there drenched in salt water.

The next day, we woke up and headed straight to the bathrooms because we were hoping that the girls hadn't left yet. We just wanted to see them one last time and I wanted to get the truth out of Nicole about the kissing ordeal. Did we both just get played by her? There were so many questions. I am over here doubting my friend and he's over there just wanting to prove he was telling the truth. After a long, silent walk we arrived at what used to be their campsite. It was of no surprise that their mothers wanted to beat the traffic heading home.

Our minds were racing, *How could they just leave us and not say goodbye? Will we ever know the truth? Did they not have as much fun as us? Will we ever see them again?*

Now it was our turn to leave and head home. This could have been a couple of days later or even hours later, this is not confirmed. We get home and automatically go for the landline. (A landline is a phone that is plugged into the wall, in case you forgot. At that time, we had no cell phones, we had no Skype, or messenger, we had no way of contacting them except by using an international calling card. As far I can remember, you would pay to add minutes to a card, then use the card to talk to an operator and somehow, magically, Canada's phone lines were activated.) Here's the catch, we only knew where she was from and a Canadian phone number has an extra four hundred and seventy-six digits to dial. We didn't even know we were supposed to use a calling card at first. Also, if I remember correctly, we were basing this phone call off of our memory of what Nicole wrote in the sand since she didn't give us her number on paper.

Why would she do that?

She wrote it in the sand and I can't, for the life of me, understand why we didn't just write it down there. I have vivid memories of looking up Canadian area codes and trying to make sense of whatever phone numbers we were trying to recall.

I actually called my grandmother because I knew I was part French on her side. However, my grandmother speaks *zero* French. Why I thought that would be an "Einstein moment" is beyond me, but I did it anyway. She laughed at me and thought it was cute when I called her to ask about Canadian area codes, and how to dial a number that had too many digits in it. As I am writing this, I want to say that we found names in the phone book that were similar, or even hers, but we could never get through.

I really don't remember what happened after Mike lied to me. I try to forget the whole event now. To be honest, for all I know, he kept Nicole's real phone number to himself and contacted her when I wasn't around. It's not something so ridiculous that it would be out the question. Now, I am just speculating. There is a part of me that actually remembers getting a hold of her but I'd have to talk to Mike and we all know how his stories end up. (Just kidding. Mike, I love you, Brother. If you ever read this, please contact me and correct this story with your angle. I know there are always two sides to a story, but I need you to also understand there can only be one *TRUE* story, my friend. Just remember that, fucker. In all seriousness, none of this would have happened without you being a great friend and inviting me up to Maine to begin with, and I truly appreciate you for that.)

Okay, moving on. Earlier, I mentioned Ryan. Ryan, to this

day, is someone I can call up and know he's there for me. It's weird, we'll go months without talking and somehow, we'll contact each other around the same time and catch up like we've been speaking the whole time. Granted, with time, things change and we've both moved a few times and what not, but the friendship hasn't disappeared by any means. He's still a great guy.

One time, at my house in Charlton, Massachusetts, we were sitting on my wicked old couch in my bedroom. It was awesome, it had turkeys on it. The arms of the couch were solid wood, so it was super duper comfortable to lean on. No, really though the couch was really comfortable. That's where my friends would sleep when we would have sleepovers. Let's try this again: We were sitting on the couch and listening to AM radio. Why the hell were we doing that? Oh, no reason at all. It was just that the Boston Red Sox were playing and at my house, we didn't have cable television. Luckily for Ryan, it was his turn for *his* parents to drive and I had slept at his house too many times that month, according to my dad. Whatever that meant.

Chill, Dad! It's the weekend.

The funny thing is, we were walking distance from each other's homes if we really couldn't get a ride. Bikes were also a great way to not waste time.

Anyways, Ryan is a huge Sox fan and we used to play little league together. Somewhere along the line, I ended up with a Red Sox program with a scorecard near the back. You are supposed to use that card when you are an attendee at the game itself, but who does that when Nomar Garciaparra is up to bat and you're watching him play with the velcro on his gloves? Ryan and I, bored out of our minds at my house, decided to listen to the game because we couldn't watch it on TV or stream it illegally online. We sat through all nine innings just listening and writing out the score as it was called. It really is a very pleasant memory in my mind.

Ryan was not on my team in little league (of course my best friend had to be yet another opponent of mine). He used to play first base, and that was *his* position. When you're young, the only position on the field you beg the coach to play is...pitcher, right? I have no idea why but we would always ask our coach to pitch, and he would always say no. Somehow, I must have begged the coach enough to pitch that he finally gave me a chance, and it just so happened to be against Ryan's team. (Crazy, right? What are the odds?) I got what every ballplayer dreamed of and it was happening in front of my best friend. I actually got to pitch to Ryan. Wait, it gets better.

This was probably my first lesson on being careful about what you wish for. I wanted to strike him out so badly, but what does he do? I throw my best pitch--which was probably about 30mph at the time--and he *crushes* it. Mind you, Ryan was not a small athletic kid around that time. He was bigger than I was and ran slower than me. Either way, to his credit he crushed my best pitch and the ball landed in between two outfielders. As I watched the ball soar over my head and into the gaping hole in deep center, it just happened to take an unexpected, slow roll, and zig-zag so much that my teammates couldn't seem to pick it up. I couldn't believe it. I was appalled. Right around this time, out of the corner of my eye, who do you think is rounding first base? I swear to you, I have never seen Ryan run so fast in my life. It was like everything in my life at that moment was in extremely slow motion, or even still, and the only thing I saw was Ryan flying at the speed of light.

The center fielder finally found the little ghost he was chasing around and picked it up, but by this time Ryan was rounding third. Have you ever seen a twelve-year-old throw a baseball from deep center field to home plate accurately? Let alone, from center to home without a cut-off? *NO*, of course not. Ryan touched third base and could have practically walked to home plate with a smile on his face, that's how far away this ball was from getting him out. He scored an in-the-park home run. Off of me!

That's not something I try to think about often, but it comes up every time I think of little league and Ryan. He was such a good sport though, I don't ever remember him rubbing it in my face, ever. He knew how much that shit hurt and he knew he hit one off me, that was enough for him. The moral of this entire chapter is:

Do NOT Trust your friends.

6

THE CHASE

I got into reading about 8 years after high school. If you are in high school or in college, don't forget to keep learning. It's up to you to find books that trigger something inside of you, and it's up to you to ask for recommendations. There are plenty of "book clubs" online that have great reads. Personally, I highly recommend experimenting. Start in finance. Start in health. Start in business. Start with biographies from the people you currently admire, and in time these selections will change. For example, if you decide, through experimentation, reading about finance really resonated with you because you learned something, look up related books on Amazon. It's that simple to get the ball rolling. You will move forward with each book you attempt to read or fully complete. Either way, it's a win for you. Knowledge is power.

Of course, maybe reading isn't for you. Maybe watching videos online is a better way for you to learn. There are no right and wrong ways to learn. JUST LEARN!

The quest for knowledge is probably the number one motivator in my life. In school, I had a hard time understanding things if they were not spelled out to me, as plain as day. This became a problem because teachers would have a time sensitive curriculum and they wouldn't be able to spend time with me specifically on a problem that stumped me. It just took time, that was all I needed. I needed time and someone to teach me on my own time.

I believe if you have the knowledge and someone does not, you should share your wealth of understanding because we all know how frustrating it is when you just can't grasp why it's done a certain way.

Over the years, I have had to teach myself how to do many, many things in order to survive. I started working at a young age when I wanted to go to the movies and hang out with friends. Occasionally my parents could afford it but not very often. One of my first jobs was raking leaves in the fall. I learned fairly quickly that raking leaves left you with blisters on your hands when you worked at a swift pace. I also realized that your annual income is about $600. Once you clean up all the leaves, you have no more work.

I'm not the kind of person that *leaves* a pile in the yard for tomorrow...no pun intended. Alright, maybe it was intended a little bit. I refer to those type of jokes as "Dad jokes." Am I right?

"Dad, STOP! Please! Oh my God, you're embarrassing me."

"Come on, Buddy, did ya hear that? That was a good one. Come on."

"Yea, Dad. Hilarious."

It's funny to think about how stupid those Dad Jokes are but at the same time, how quick-witted one has to be to conjure up something so perfect.

As I was saying, when the fall ended I needed to find new work. I was doing all kinds of odd jobs like shoveling out my neighbor's driveways. I would say, "No, no, no! I'll shovel for free."

When you're twelve or thirteen years old, your neighbors aren't going to let you shovel for free. I caught on pretty quickly. This neighbor, that neighbor, and I could buy new toy model cars to build. I could even go to the movies, finally. Money was making me pretty happy.

Again, shoveling by itself, is not a stable career choice. Even as a 13-year-old I could tell you that. So, spring came around and I started mowing my grandparent's lawn for a few dollars. After the lawn was cut, my grandfather would have to drive me home and we'd stop at Wendy's for some fuel. (Speaking of, I could really use a spicy chicken sandwich right now.)

I could go out and get money anywhere. The only place I couldn't find money was at my own house. If I remember correctly, my parents tried an allowance for a little while because I kept saying, "All my friends have one!"

You can tell I never really got an allowance because I don't know the kind of things one must do to make money from their parents.

My friends would be like, "Aw, Dude, let's go to Ronnie's for some ice cream."

I'd be so confused. "Where did you *get* this money? I know

you spent *your* twenty bucks *last* night because you had to pay for *me!*"

"Oh, I just did the dishes."

"WHAT? Is that it? I had to go pick up my dog's shit. Then, water the garden, cut the grass, move three cords of wood, stack it, move it back, and then light the wood stove...and this was all after I did the dishes *too*, ya dick!"

I was always up to something labor intensive. The constant hustle never seemed to end. It might sound crazy, but I actually enjoyed working with my hands, walking a lawn mower, and cutting grass. That's probably the number one reason I was so tan all the time. That and sports.

Just after I made the varsity baseball team my junior year, and read my name on that piece of paper taped to the painted cinder blocks, I was told that I needed to get a real job in order to make money. My family and I weren't ballers and I was the oldest of four children, so I was determined to make my family proud and set a good example for my younger siblings. For the first time in my life, I was about to feel what it was like to give up something that made you happy for something that would make me a couple of dollars an hour so I could afford my own yearbook and suit for prom.

One of my first jobs, on the books, was washing dishes in the back of a fast-food seafood restaurant around the age of fourteen or fifteen. I was eventually promoted to helping the owner hand-cut French fries in the basement of the establishment after mopping the floors and taking out the trash. Because my parents taught us how to clean and take the trash out properly, this helped me get promoted to the fryolator. My first reaction was admittedly a bit sarcastic, *Lucky me,* I thought, *Yippy! I get to learn how to boil grease.*

Next to the fryolators, there was a grill and my bosses thought the time had come for me to learn how to use it. I moved to the front of the restaurant and began interacting with customers and employees. Not only did it teach me how to make a mean grilled chicken sandwich, but it also taught me how to work my way up the ladder of an establishment that I had no desire to be a part of. The bosses never seemed to appreciate my accomplishments, they never patted me on the back when they promoted me, it was just expected of me. It was expected of me to work my way up for a wage that increased incrementally over time. The "rest of my life" was already sounding like I would never find happiness.

This sucks! I thought, *A little "Thank You," would be nice from time to time.*

While I was working at Ronnie's Seafood, I was also attending Bay Path which was a vocational high school. One week of academics--that covered two weeks worth of academics--and then one week in shop. The name of the shop that taught me a trade was called, Cabinet and Millwork. Not to be confused with rough carpentry, this was finish carpentry. Not a hack job. That shop would teach me how to build furniture, kitchen cabinets, shelves, houses, and anything else you could make out of wood. The school would teach you how to get a job in a great company, with great benefits, and how to work your way up a ladder in a corporation like that. It was my first pick out of all the exploratories.

After nine exploratories, basically experimenting with nine different career options, I had to make a tough decision. At the time, I just knew that if I had to pick a career that I would be stuck with for the rest of my life, I would have to do something that I kind of enjoyed doing. At thirteen, I was forced to make a decision that forty-year-olds still can't make. How was I supposed to know what I wanted to do for the rest of my life at thirteen years old? That's a pretty overwhelming decision to force a kid to make. Nonetheless, I made the decision and I have to say that carpentry has gotten me out of so much shit in my life that I have to thank the younger me for making that decision. I am pretty stoked that I didn't get stuck with small engines.

My teachers could see I fully understood how to work with wood and they recommended that I apply for a woodworking job as soon as possible, so I did. At Bay Path you could actually work in the real world, every other week, starting halfway through junior year. It was an amazing way to make money while I was attending high school. One of my teachers told me he knew a guy that he could talk to and put in a good word for me.

Since I lived right up the road from Ronnie's Seafood in Charlton, Massachusetts, I could walk to work after school. There was no need for a car just yet. I was working at Ronnie's and raking leaves and shoveling, all while trying to save all my pennies to go to Maine during the summers. I needed spending money. With four kids, my parents couldn't afford to give us all spending money every time we went on vacation with our friends. It was a good thing I was working.

In 2006, I was talking to a kid at Ronnie's and he told me that he was selling a 1990 Lincoln Continental that he had repaired. I knew this deal wouldn't last forever and I needed to make enough money to buy it. The issue was that I wanted it then and there. I told my grandparents about it and if I'm not mistaken, they paid for a lot of it. I think the kid was asking for $1,200 or something like that. My Grandparents fronted the money and I had to pay them back, obviously. They knew I was working and trying to get a co-op job through the school, so their investment wouldn't go to waste. They knew I was good for it.

It was right around that time when I got my permit. Even though Ronnie's was within walking distance, you better believe I drove a quarter of a mile just to park it there and look at it while I was taking out the trash.

Look at my new car! Damn, she's pretty! I'd say to myself.

Halfway through my junior year, one of my shop teachers set me up with an interview. In the spring of 2007, I applied to Blue Hive, which was a company that built exhibits for trade shows. I had no idea what trade shows were but they said they needed younger talent. By younger talent, they just meant someone that knew their way around a dustpan and brush.

Here we go again! Starting at the bottom.

Blue Hive gave me a job and I was making the most money I had ever made, about $9.00 per hour. The minimum wage in 2007 was $7.25 and that was exactly what Ronnie's was still paying me after promoting me. Maybe it was a few cents more but it was still pennies, so I was in heaven. *$9.00 an hour?* I thought.

That was more money than any one of my friends were making. I was finally making a decent wage. It meant a lot to me because growing up happened rather quickly for me. I wouldn't say my family was "no food on the table" kind of poor, but we never seemed to have any money.

For instance, just to put it into perspective for you, one of my friends had a dirt bike. One had a quad, which is also a dirt bike with double the amount of wheels. Some of my friends had in-ground pools. Some of my friends had central AC. Some friends had motor-homes or campers as well. Some friends went to Disney World...every year! Some would go to concerts all the time. Some of my peers didn't have to worry about buying their own student yearbook or renting a suit for prom because their parents could afford it.

I had this one friend, *had* is the key word, who kept making fun of me because every time he slept over, we would either have an off brand of Cheerios *or* an off-brand of Corn Flakes.

My mother would empty the gigantic bag of cereal into an even bigger plastic container. I still think she did it to hide the fact that they weren't "real cereals" as we used to call them. My father would always empty the remainder of one "fake cereal" into a container freshly filled with the newest "fake cereal." Of course, just trying to consolidate the amount of visibly mismatched Tupperware. Which I hated.

Don't mix my Goddamn cereal, Dad! You just ruined everything.

That was it. Life was over for me.

When you have four kids as my parents did, they were obviously trying to keep the cost of groceries down. Three growing boys and one growing girl tend to eat whatever is in the kitchen cabinets. I remember opening up the cupboards multiple times in less than 30 minutes. I would do this just to see if the shelves had magically restocked themselves, without me having to throw on my Starter sneakers from Walmart to help my mom bring in two hundred and forty-five plastic bags from BJ's.

In my home town, we never had a grocery store. The other

day, one of my best friends from childhood reminded me that our parents had to travel twenty to thirty minutes to pick up some groceries. I didn't believe him. I totally forgot about how small my town was. By the time I was old enough to buy my own "real cereal" we had moved to a town that had grocery stores. When I think about it, I remember stopping at my buddy's house after school and then grabbing groceries on the way home in another town. We definitely always had food on the table. My parents might have had trouble providing the food but they never let us see that. That being said, it was nice to finally be able to eat whatever I wanted to eat, whenever I wanted, because I was the one paying for it.

Now that I had a real job, I had to figure out what to do with Ronnie's. My boss was actually offended when I told him that I found a real job every other week. He thought grilling and dropping fries was my future. He was wrong. I stuck it out a little longer at Ronnie's and worked both jobs because I was determined to pay my grandparents back.

My boss at Blue-Hive offered me more hours than I was allowed to work through the school, so I would work on vacations and holidays. Sometimes, if they were working late one evening, I would go straight from school on an academic week and work for a few hours after school. This was not supposed to happen because Bay Path wanted to make sure their students weren't getting overworked and that their academic skill set was up to par, but I wanted more money and at the time, more money meant having to work more hours. The trade show industry has more hours to pick up that you can imagine. If you want to work, you got it. There were so many deadlines that needed to be hit, you couldn't work enough. My boss and I decided to fudge the time sheet I was required to deliver after each co-op week. Seeing how the time sheets were filled out with a pencil and handed in by hand, it wasn't very hard to say that I worked the maximum amount of hours that Bay Path allowed. I'd actually be working double or triple the hours but that wasn't any of their business if I was still completing all my work on time.

Jumping ahead, my 1990 Lincoln Continental wouldn't start after school one day. I walked out to my car and was on my way to work, or so I thought, and it wouldn't start. This wasn't long after I bought it and paid off my debt. I was in trouble because I needed to get to my new job and I didn't want them firing me soon after they had hired me.

Later on that day or week, I convinced my mother to take me to a car dealership because I wanted a new car and not a pre-owned, half-repaired clunker. We arrived at Hyundai and I found a 2008 Elantra that I wanted to buy. It only had 8 miles on it. I don't know how I did it, but my mom felt bad enough to persuade my dad to co-sign a loan for it.

BOOM!

Once again, I got the one thing I focused on acquiring. The car loan was listed in my father's name and I didn't want to mess up his credit. I didn't even know what credit was at the time, but it seemed important to him. The bank said I needed to make 6 months worth of payments on time and they would transfer the loan into my name so I could start building my own credit. That sounded like something I could handle. I wasn't financially educated but I knew that my job would cover most of the car payment and I figured I would be okay.

I *would* have been fine if I hadn't gotten into trouble leaving school shortly after I bought my new car. My brother, Pete, was in the back seat and in the passenger seat sat my high school sweetheart. (I was driving her home.) As I followed my buddy around a corner and over a little hill, I noticed a cop charging at me in the center of the street, waving at me to pull over. On the right-hand side of the street, I saw my buddy pulled over already. The cop had a radar gun that he was just holding in his hand, aiming at nothing. As I pulled in behind my buddy, Mike, the cop comes over to my window and tells me to roll down my window. At the time, I was a little punk and I rolled the window down just enough to slide fingers over the glass but not a wrist.

"Roll the window down!" He said, "And turn off the music!"

I was blasting music and loving every minute of it because we just got out of school for the day.

He started asking questions that I tried to answer truthfully but failed miserably, "How old are you?"

"I'm sixteen and a half...I'm seventeen...seventeen," I said.

The issue was that I was not supposed to be driving anyone under the age of twenty-one unless they had their license for three years already or were members of my family. This was because I was sixteen and a half and I had just gotten my license. I needed to have my license for a year in order to drive anyone else. Of course, I knew this all too well but I was trying to play it cool in front of my high school sweetheart, and I was trying to impress my younger brother, being the oldest and all.

The cop asked for my license and I knew, right then and there, that I was totally fucked.

"Step out of the car!" He said, "And turn off your music, damn it!"

Still feeling like a rebel, I said, "Why?"

"Listen, you little shit, get the fuck outta the car. RIGHT NOW!" This guy wasn't having any of it.

Apparently, my brother wasn't having it either.

He said, "Don't talk to my brother like that! Who do you think you are? There's a lady in the car! Stop being a dick!"

As my brother opened the door, "Pete, chill! It's okay--" I started to say.

"No! It's not okay. This dude's being a dick to you. Fuck that!"

The cop asked Pete, "Who are you?"

Poor kid. He was 14 years old and just trying to help me. Besides being family, I don't really know what made him do this, but I appreciated it. He used a power move on the cop, got out of the car and started to walk around towards the cop.

Standing tall and proud, "My name is Peter Danna. I'm part of the police explorers and..."

"Not anymore you're not!" Said the cop, as he cut him off.

Pete started pleading, "What the fuck? What do you mean?"

"I will personally make sure you are not part of the police explorers anymore." The cop said.

That was it. Pete was done, and it was all my fault. That's not all, because I was such a dick back in the day and I was trying to get away with all kinds of shit, it caught up to me. After handing me a summons, the officer let me drive away without towing my car. I don't know why but I think he was so frustrated with Pete that he just wanted us out of his hair. Then he could finish what he started with my friend, Mike, who was still pulled over up ahead of us.

I had to tell my parents about what had happened because if I lost my license, I would need a ride to work in order to pay for the car I was no longer able to drive. I arrived at court about a month later and spoke to the court magistrate.

He asked, "It says here that you were speeding. Is that true?"

I knew for a fact that I wasn't speeding and that was the truth. "No, Sir."

"What happened?"

"Well, I was coming over the hill and the officer was in the middle of the street, charging at my car, waving his hands for me to pull over. He had just pulled my friend over."

"Okay. It says he detected you were speeding with his radar gun. Is that false, too?"

"I know this sound ridiculous, Sir, but I wasn't speeding and he has no proof that I was speeding because his gun wasn't even pointing at me. Also, I slammed on my brakes on the top of the hill because I saw him charging at my car, waving for me to pull over. There was no time for him to register my speed." I said.

"Okay. Listen, I'll let you go on the speeding ticket, okay? However, you were driving people that were not supposed to be in your car, correct?"

"Well, yes and no!"

"How's that?"

"I was able to drive my brother but not my girlfriend."

"Okay. So, again, you were driving someone you weren't supposed to have in the car, correct?" He was very stern.

Defeated, I replied, "Yes. That's correct."

Then it occurred to me that if I wasn't speeding, I should

have never gotten pulled over, to begin with. That means that he would have never known who I had in the car. That means the cop is at fault.

I decided to test my luck, "Sir, if I wasn't speeding, then why did he pull me over? If he wrongly pulled me over, then everything that happened after his fault should be void."

Not having any of that, "That's not how it works, Isaac. I will let you off of the speeding ticket but I'm suspending your license for sixty days."

"But, Sir, I..."

"That's it. Have a good day!" He said.

FUCK! I thought, *Now I have to talk to Dad!*

Talking to Dad was never going to end well and no matter how the conversation went, I was still going to have to sit right next to him, every morning, on the car ride to work. That's exactly what happened. Every other week that fell within the next sixty days, my dad had to drive my punk ass to work and drop me off on the way to his job. Luckily, if we are looking at the positives, it literally was on the way and I was able to get a lot of overtime pay because I was working on my dad's schedule. This allowed me to save up a little bit of money and it also allowed me to keep paying for *my* car, that my *dad* was now driving back and forth to work. Technically, it was under his name anyways, so I couldn't make a comment about him racking up the miles.

When they saw that I was willing to do anything to get to work, Blue Hive offered me a fulltime job after I graduated in the summer of 2008. I took the job, and I was promised a raise when I signed on but never got one. With all the traveling around, dating young ladies in other states, attending photo shoots and acting classes, I needed more money. It always seemed to be about money. Money for this, money for that. Where was it? I had a fulltime job that gave me plenty of overtime but it still didn't seem like enough. Maybe it was because Ronnie's wouldn't work with me on a schedule for the evenings and I ended up having to leave. What did I do? Worked more over time.

Once again, because I showed them how much I wanted to work, they promoted me to a CNC machine. The CNC position was paying the same wage as my position before, but I was expected to learn something new in addition to what I already knew, and then apply it. After a year of that, I decided to tell my foreman about the fact that I was promised a raise by the former foreman. Obviously, this new guy didn't believe me and decided that conversation was not going to happen any time soon and kicked me out of his office. That fucker hated me so much. I just hated how he treated us and how much work he expected us to do. It was almost as if he had never worked as a builder himself and had this magical time frame he assumed everything would be finished by. It just wasn't the case.

I tried again. I said, "Okay, I need a raise. I looked on Craigslist and with the skills that I have acquired recently, running the CNC machine and all, I can be getting paid upwards of $20/hr."

Not phased at all, he said, "Isaac, a fucking monkey could do your job."

I promise that is exactly what he said to me.

Now I was pissed. "Okay, fine. Let's see if you can go get a monkey to do my job!"

"Is that a threat?"

"Not at all. I'll be back."

I nicely walked out of his office and headed right into the owner's office. This guy was as high up as I could get. I jumped right over the other three people that could have relayed this message, but enough was enough.

After my gentle knock, "Come in, Isaac."

"Hey, Paul! How are you?" I asked.

"I'm doing well. How can I help you?" He said, in his political style.

"Okay, I was promised a raise before our companies merged and now I have a new boss. He won't listen to me and said that a monkey could do my job. I looked online and I found a position just down the road for almost double my wage. I love working here but I really need the extra money and I've been waiting for a long time."

"Isaac, we'll get it sorted out. I'll talk to Lenny."

I left his office thinking, *See? How fucking hard was that?*

Next thing I knew, my foreman comes wobbling over to me and asks, "You went over my head to get a raise after I told you that wasn't an option?"

He was so pissed off, it was incredible. It was the ultimate display of disrespect for this man.

"Yes, I did! Paul said he was going to work it out." I said with a little shit eating grin on my face.

"Yeah, Lenny wants to talk to you. Don't do that again!" He said.

Still smirking, "Thanks! I gotta get back to work now."

All the guys in the shop were watching this altercation take place and they all wanted to know what happened after the conversation was over. The guys I worked with were all like fathers to me. Each had their own way of communicating and each had their own way of how things were done. In their minds, their way was the best after years of trial and error. They were amazing mentors when it came to woodworking and exhibit building.

Sure enough, Lenny hooked me up with a few dollars more per hour and I was as happy as a clam. For the time being. It was around that time that the guys started showing me how to assemble and disassemble entire booths because I was offered a sweet little gig that I had yet to try. They wanted me to stand in for a guy that had been traveling the United States with clients and booths, setting them up and tearing them down when the shows were over. I was just a broke eighteen year old from a small town and I was about to fly all the way to Anaheim, California. I had never been out west before, but for a long time, I had been dreaming about Hollywood. I knew those two cities were not close to one another but I wanted to see Hollywood more than anything.

I had become friends with an actor, through Facebook, just before I was asked to go to Anaheim. At Blue Hive, I had two weeks of vacation time I could use so I decided to save my money and plan my Hollywood trip around my work trip. I asked Jack, the vice president of the company, who I would be accompanied by on this trip if I could extend the length of the trip, but use the two flights that were included with work. He said that would be fine but he warned me that Hollywood was not a nice place.

My friend, from Facebook, who I had never met before in my life, was going to drive from Hollywood to Anaheim and pick me up after the trade show had started and my job was complete. Everyone knew about this trip and they thought I was fucking nuts.

"Let me get this straight, you're going to meet a kid that you've never met before, and you're going to stay with him for an entire week?" They'd ask.

"That's the plan!" I'd say.

Friends and family were not even close to as happy about it as I was. To me, Waldo was a genuine guy, we had the same interests, and he was about to be my tour guide. I wasn't thinking anything else about it. In addition to exploring Hollywood, he promised he would take me to Las Vegas and he would show me around there as well. Apparently, he and his friends would travel back and forth, through the mountains, every so often and stay for a weekend. It just seemed too good to be true to everyone around me. They all thought Waldo was going to try and get into my pants or want more in return for letting me stay with him. I thought nothing of that. Even if he did want to be gay lovers, I was (and still am) a straight male with a strong sense of self-confidence. I wasn't worried at all, but I was starting to get annoyed with everyone making the same stupid jokes about dicks and buttholes. That just pushed me to leave and explore the west coast even more after not feeling the support of my friends. See, my friends and family had never seen California and I could see they were actually kind of jealous that I got a chance to go.

The time had come. We packed the booth and sent it out. The next morning, around four thirty, a black car pulled up to my house and took me to the airport. I felt like royalty. Tired, but royalty. I remember the sun rising as we drove into Logan Airport, in Boston. I had flown before but only to see my grandparents in Florida, so it was a little nerve racking when I found that we were about to have a six and a half hour flight since the longest flight I had been on was about three hours. We landed at John Wayne Airport near Laguna Beach and I remember stepping off of the plane in the middle of the runway. It was so weird. It rained so little there, that they didn't need to hook us up to one of those long, accordion-like, alleyways. I'll never forget walking down the steps, seeing palm trees, and breathing in dry heat in the middle of the day.

Jack brought his assistant, Jessica, to help me out when he had to entertain clients and more important shit than telling an eighteen-year-old what to do. Jessica and I waited as Jack came back from the car rental desk and he flashed us the keys and said, "Look for an Audi convertible!"

Did he just say Audi convertible? I thought.

Sure enough, we found the Audi and tried to pack three suitcases into the trunk but I ended up having to squeeze in the back seat with most of our luggage. That was the least of my problems at that moment. I was in California.

Jack said, "Isaac, I think we're going to head to Laguna Beach this afternoon and catch the sunset there while we have some dinner. How's that sound?"

"How's that sound? That sounds fucking awesome!" I said.

"I thought you'd like that!"

ZOOM!

Top down, sun beating down, new Black Eyed Peas music on the radio, fresh out of the studio, we sped out of the rental lot and hopped on a ten-lane highway. Our hotel was in Anaheim but we arrived half a day early. Jack and Jess wanted to show me what California looked like. We drove through The Hills area, down Laguna Canyon Road, and it was something straight out of the television shows. I only knew about The Hills but had never watched much of it. I remember it started to sprinkle while we were driving and we almost had to pull over and raise the soft top.

"Of course, the only time of year when it rains out here, we're driving a convertible," Jack said.

While we were eating, the sun was setting and all I could think about was that I had watched the sun rise as far east as I could go and at that moment I was watching the sun set, as far west as possible. I had never experienced the sun setting on what appeared to be the edge of the world. It was so insane. I witnessed the sun rise and set on shimmering horizons three thousand miles apart from each other.

I set the booth up and worked my ass off for a week. After the trade show was over in Anaheim, I called Waldo and had him pick me up. He showed me a sweet pizza place that I had never seen before, called California Pizza Kitchen. I literally thought that place was exclusively in Cali because I had never seen one before. Coming to find out, it was just another chain. Waldo and I got along really well. We were laughing and having a blast.

We hopped back up into his Jeep and drove to Las Vegas. Let me tell you, one of my favorite memories is when we drove through the mountains and out of nowhere, a city in the desert appeared. The funniest part was that when we arrived, I couldn't do anything because I was just 18 years old. What did we do instead of gambling or walking through casinos? I'm glad you asked. We literally just went and saw a movie.

Since there wasn't much else to do in Vegas for an 18-year-old at the time, we decided to head back to Hollywood. I was so excited, I couldn't control myself. He showed me around and we went to a club and grabbed some fancy sushi from a famous sushi bar. I was so far from home and exploring the west coast all by myself with a friend. This was unreal to me. LA wasn't what I thought it was going to be. Hollywood was basically garbage and I didn't see myself staying there.

Also, before I left to Cali, I had just slept with the love of my life who told me that she wanted me to stay and never leave. Obviously, this was just pillow talk but that is probably the main reason I wasn't enjoying the west coast like I should have been at the time. We agreed that when I came back, we would be with each other. It was literally all I could think about and I missed her like crazy, so I told Waldo I wanted to fly back early and I called Jack to ask him to change my flights. That's how bad I missed her and how much I wanted to be with her. The flight felt like it was taking years to get anywhere. When I arrived in Logan, guess who I texted first? Guess who never responded. She never responded to my text that I had sent her 6 hours prior before the flight took off. I was pissed. She had been texting me while I was away and she told me she wanted me just as bad as I wanted her. This wasn't adding up.

Apparently, she never ended up breaking up with her boyfriend. This kid was a piece of shit and now I was even lower than he was for just being a booty call and fucking some other dude's girl. I thought they had either ended things or were in the middle of ending things because that was what I was being told. At the time, I was definitely a piece of shit anyway, because I should have never even tried to be with her knowing she had someone else in the picture. Back then I didn't care. He never even got up out of bed on Valentine's day. What kind of man does that? You're not a man if you don't put time aside for your lady on the days that mean the most to her. What I didn't realize is that I wasn't a man either because I was fooling around with someone's lady. I deserved everything I got.

After that, I focused on myself and really tried to eliminate interruptions. This meant working as many hours as I could at my job and saving as much money as I could to move away from home. I really didn't want to be around that situation anymore. I wanted to be famous and I was determined to move back to California now. Even though I didn't even enjoy it while I was there the first time. As I was saving, I met a photographer that was moving to NYC not long after I met her. She was older than I was and we had some fun on a mature level. Friends with benefits kind of thing. That's all it could be because I was determined to move to Cali as soon as possible. Then she moved to NYC.

I was attending acting classes in Boston and driving to auditions in NYC every few weeks. I loved it there. The grandeur, the people, the energy, the architecture, it was for me. At the time I was just trying to avoid traffic going back and forth so I never really thought about moving there. I spoke to my best friend, Justin, and we had decided that we would both move to California. The only issue was that he had a girlfriend and they were expecting a child. This meant that I wasn't going to be having the kind of fun I wanted to have and that I was going to lose my best friend for a little while to fatherhood. I understood this though and was okay with it. I didn't have a choice. I decided to look at housing and tried finding jobs in California. Then my photographer lady friend told me that she was loving New York and that I would too.

I started looking at acting schools in New York City and I

tried to find a job that was similar to building trade show exhibits but most of them weren't hiring. Now we had a problem. I needed to find housing, a job, and a school.

Then it clicked, *"I wonder if there is an acting college that has dorms?"*

Sure enough, I found a few and figured out how to apply. I started saving more money and found a part-time hustle. The hustle consisted of buying large amounts of weed and selling smalls amounts to smokers. No joke, I saved enough to buy myself a MacBook Pro, a backpack, and still had $3,000 in my bank. It was fucking amazing.

When it was time to decide on locations for schools, it was between Hollywood and NYC. I kept playing both of the school's sales videos. I played them over and over again. Every day I would just watch those videos and hype myself up. Then I decided to audition in NYC and found that I could pick a campus after I was accepted. I called up my only NYC friend who was actually from MA and she said I could crash with her for the weekend while I auditioned for the acting schools. Somehow, I was able to audition for two schools in one trip to NYC. I really don't remember how I worked that out.

My lady friend had been out there for a few months now and she promised to show me around on my visit. She kept telling me that I wouldn't want to move to LA after I had actually experienced the city the way someone's supposed to. I took a Peter Pan bus down and linked up with her the night before my first audition. She and her friends welcomed me with open arms as we ate dinner under Highline Park as the sun set over the Hudson River. It was magical--way better than Cali. From there we ventured into Brooklyn and she took me to some bar that allowed people to sit out on the sidewalk and drink. I didn't drink that night because I had my first audition the next day and I wanted to give it everything I had. I knew what was at stake here.

The audition came and went, and I felt like I nailed it. The guy that auditioned me was from Boston and he asked me where I wanted to go if I got accepted. I told him that I'd like to go to LA. He told me that he thought I'd really make a good fit in NYC. At the time, it was funny that he said that because the night before was actually changing my mind about Los Angeles. I was purely basing this decision off of what my gut was telling me to do this time, I wasn't basing it off of anyone's promises or opinions like I did last time.

I woke up the next day and took the subway back into the city to audition for school number two. I nailed that one too, I just felt it. I told my New York friend, that I was changing my mind about LA.

She laughed as she said, "I told you!"

She was right. It was incredible. I hopped back on the bus to head back to MA and ended up cuddling with an older gentleman that started chatting me up.

Damn those seats were tight!

I was explaining how I had these auditions and how I was torn between LA and NYC. He was laughing and persuading me to move to NYC based on how I was telling him what I felt for each city.

After I got back home, I had to get back to work on Monday and keep making that money in case I got accepted. I went to pick up another pound or two of weed so I could make money a little faster. When I say a little faster, I mean a lot faster.

I parked and walked up to the door of the house that my dealer lived in. This house was huge. It was an old Victorian home that my dealer and a minimum of five of his friends lived in to grow weed for a living. Usually, the door was answered in a matter of seconds because these dudes were so paranoid all the time. I learned so much from them because they really believed that weed helped people and so on and so forth. I just saw it as an opportunity to make some serious money to move.

Nobody answered the door. Now if you have ever seen any kind of movie or show, ever, you know that cannot be a good sign. Something wasn't adding up.

Fuck that noise!

I hopped in my car and explained to all my customers that I was no longer in business due to a change in my location. It took no time at all for me to realize that I needed to stop that shit right then and there, so I did. It just meant that I had to work more over time. That was a small price to pay if I got away with dealing for a little while.

Lesson one, know when to fold. A few weeks later, I received my acceptance letters from BOTH schools. That was one of the best moments of my life. I had to choose between two acting colleges in a matter of weeks after I had decided that that's what I really wanted to do. I played them both and tried to work down the cost of tuition. It worked a little bit but not as much as I had hoped. Either way, it didn't matter. I designed my future and made my dream a reality. I know that sounds cheesy but I swear that is exactly what I did. That's where it all began for me.

7

MOVING TO NEW YORK CITY

When my parents walked over to their car after hugging
and kissing me goodbye back in September 2011, I
knew I was fucked. As I looked up, I could only see glass;
windows, streetlights, and balconies blocked out any stars if
there even were any in the sky that night. I remember I was
standing on Lexington Ave and East 97th St. in Manhattan. It
was a beautiful moment, but at the same time, terrifying. The
Drama school that I decided to go with, was about to start in a
couple of days and I had to find my way to the American
Academy of Dramatic Arts. The city was so overwhelming when
I first arrived. I've got butterflies right now just thinking about
that moment. I remember having dinner with my parents and my
little brother, Joe. Then, before I knew it, they were gone.

Nobody in the city knew who I was. Nobody cared. Nobody
loved me. There were no smiles. Everyone's head was down and
they were hustling and running to wherever they needed to be.
People invaded my privacy. I was in and out of New Yorker's

lives, only inches away from my fingertips, and they didn't even know I was next to them. It's amazing how so many humans can live in such a condensed area and not give a flying fuck that there is another human being brushing up against them. Where was I? What was I doing? What genius thought this was a good idea? Dropping everything in their life to move to New York City to become "famous?"

Hey! That's me.

Man, was I in for a surprise. I cannot tell you how fast I had to learn how to walk on my own two feet. Literally. How was I suppose to find my way around when the fucking subway map looked like *it* was confused?

I thought to myself, *this must be what they meant by "Up Shit Creek Without a Paddle."*

That night, I went to bed and woke up ready to take on the world the next day.

Bring it on, bitch!

My naivety got the best of me at the beginning. Walking around with a Boston Red Sox hat and tee shirt like I had never even heard of the Yankees.

Who? Are they even in the MLB?

No, seriously though, I was smiling at everyone. I would interrupt their day by saying, "Good Morning. Hi. How are you?"

Nodding my head to everyone I saw got pretty exhausting after a while. Within the first day, I caught on to that. There was an unbelievable amount of people, no two the same. I'd never seen anything like it.

I made my way to TD Bank. I liked the colors and their branding. In all honesty, that is the only reason I stopped there first. It was pretty to look at and very eye-catching to me. To open an account they made me sit on a comfy seat and wait. My Hometown bank in Massachusetts never had these lines or couches to sit on, so I thought it was pretty cool. As I was sitting on the couch, there was a young lady that sat next to me. She was pretty, and she was also smiling. Come to think about it, after living there for ages, it was just a sign of courtesy. At the time, I thought she wanted to talk. What did I do? I introduced myself and started talking to her. I was so excited. Meeting new strangers and making friends. (You already know how well I do that.) I can only imagine what she was thinking. It must have looked like I had a "Life Is Good" Tee shirt wrapped around my head and the graphic was just cover my face.

Sometimes, even today, that's how I feel. I hope I give off that much energy still. I hope you feel it through my writing. If not, read something else. No, if not, I need to get your feedback and write another book.

We shook hands and went our separate ways after I became a new man with a new bank account. At the time, I had never even heard of TD Bank, so it was truly a fresh start. I could check my balance, digitally, online. This was perfect because right before I moved to NYC, I bought a brand new MacBook Pro with my "drug dealing, kingpin money," I discussed earlier. I am using the same laptop right now, six years later. Well done, Apple.

I was on my way to the next big thing. The rest of that day was filled with meeting new people. Before I even arrived in New York, the school had organized a Facebook group for the new class that would be attending in the fall, which was great. Before I moved I bought my Mac and it had a camera in it. (What? That was so crazy back then.) Coming from a poor household that was lacking in the tech department, it was so unreal to me. I figured it would be an excellent way to keep in touch with my family back home. This being said, I had Skyped and started vlogging within the group. Vlogging wasn't even close to a thing yet. I was ahead of the curve and I didn't even know it. I had only just come off of Myspace. Seriously. You might not even know what that is.

Since I had interacted with some of my future peers before I had arrived, I knew where their dorms were and that they would be exploring the city. Obviously, I would have to figure out how to use the subway at this point, there was really no other way around it. I didn't want to spend my hard-earned drug money on a cab just yet. I didn't even know where to grocery shop yet. It was crazy. I made my way over to West 34th St and 8th Ave just in time to order food at a diner near The New Yorker Hotel. The hotel housed a lot of students because they were smart enough to rent out entire floors for students from all over the globe. Do you want to talk about being thrown into the heart of the city? Oh, man. That was crazy. I thought my area was nuts.

If you ever get the chance to walk down 34th street, don't. Totally, kidding. Take that opportunity and prepare yourself for all the people that will just run you over on the way to their boring ass 9-5 in midtown. It really is quite an exhilarating experience and I wouldn't trade it for the world.

My classmates were patiently waiting for me in the diner. It was so refreshing to see that they too, had smiles on their faces. It was quite pleasant just meeting new people and learning about where they were from. I swear the American Academy of Dramatic Arts was anything but American. These new students were from Canada, New Castle, Scotland, Norway, Paris,

London, and so many other countries. I felt out of place, I could barely even understand the redhead from New Castle. Her name was Billie Aken-Tyers, and she was such a trip. We became great friends right off the bat. Immediately, I was introduced to British humour. Humour, not humor. I have been corrected several times on the spelling.

"We created our language before you fucked off for freedom." She'd say.

Oh yeah, she was brutal. I love her. Over the years we have ended up going separate ways but not after having her and a few foreign friends over for an American Thanksgiving just a few months after we met. Ready for the best part? There were three Brits that attended Thanksgiving that year and we all sat down and watched *The Patriot*, out of all the movies. I still crack up laughing at how times change and how we can sit, amicably, with whom we once waged war with. That ought to make you think a little bit.

Then there was Conor Ling who was a Canadian kid who ended up having some serious guitar skills. He's the one who introduced me to Poutine. According to Wiki, Poutine is a Quebecois dish popular across Canada, made with French fries and cheese curds, topped with a light brown gravy. How fucking good does that sound? There were a couple of Americans there as well but I was so intrigued by these new accents and their stories, I just didn't care about our people. Boring!

After lunch, Billie guided us to Central Park. I now know that she was guiding us North, well, technically North East and Uptown but you would never say North East. We walked straight up 8th Ave and hit the park. At the time I was so lost just trusting that she knew her way around this place. She had gotten there a few days prior to my arrival so I had no reason to doubt her exploration expertise. It didn't take long for me to learn that I needed 3 jobs just to cover the cost of a Goddamn spicy hotdog in Central Park. Most of my "drug money" was spent on food and alcohol when I first moved to the city.

September just so happens to be the month of my birth. Coincidentally, in 2011, I was turning twenty-one.

Twenty-one in NYC?

Come on, I had no parents telling me what to do or what not to do. No rules, no anything, just pure freedom...until the money ran out, of course. Once that happened, reality set in quicker than I was anticipating. It was time to start looking for a job.

8

THE JOB

After the money ran out I needed to find some way to make an income. I promised my grandmother that I would pay for these student loans and I would do whatever it took. My grandparents were the ones that co-signed my student loan for The American Academy Of Dramatic Arts. Grandma never swears and this is exactly what she told me after she signed the paperwork, "You fuck me, I'll kill you!"

So, I knew she was serious. Some people freak out about shit like that. In my head, it was only a little bit of ink on paper and I couldn't understand what the big deal was. It was and still is a big deal to them. Different generations is all. That being said, because it was such a big deal to both of us I was so thankful that they signed the loans with me so I could chase my dreams. Letting them down was not an option now and it never was. My goal was to make them proud.

After I drank away my last five bucks holding a pint of Magner's Cider in my hand, it was then that I realized I had to get my shit together. Even though drinking till I couldn't stand, waking up with a pounding headache, and staying in bed all day complaining about my life was a blast and I couldn't wait to do it again, it was time to wake the fuck up.

Since it was a drama school, there was a production department in the basement of the building. Constructed in 1907, it was the original home of the Colony Club and even though AADA had renovated it, they kept it historical in so many ways. They also used every inch of space to create that drama school. For example, the deeper you went into the basement, you would start to realize that you were standing in what used to be an in-ground pool. That is where all the props are held for all the plays. There used to be a small track for running, that wrapped around the top of one of the theatres. I can't remember what the theatre used to be but I'm assuming some sort of gym. The track is currently being used to house all the set pieces, and because it's high up and you can see down into the theatre, the old gym had been converted into a stage and part of the track is used to control all the lights, and sound design.

I only found all of this out because I walked down into the basement the very next day, after my binge drinking, and handed in my woodworking resume. I figured I was going to be the only professional finish carpenter and builder in the school. So, why would I not get that job? Sure enough, I was correct. I walked down and dropped off my resumé and began my interview for a set building position. The production designer was so fucking happy that he found someone who he could just hand projects off to. He was excited and couldn't wait for me to start.

By the time I went to NYC, I had four years of experience under my belt when it came to design and production, and I made sure to remind my future boss that I knew what I was doing. Apparently, I was quite convincing. At the time, I had no idea that he was gay and actually just wanted eye candy around for a little while. I found that out after I was hired. Not in a bad way, it was never awkward or anything. I am a firm believer that compliments are compliments wherever they are coming from. My experience with male modeling and gay photographers really made me comfortable with myself, as a straight man, to accept compliments and innuendos all the time. I mean, it can be quite annoying when they are basically begging you to play for the other team, but it's life. You want to play the fame game? You work around it.

Back to what I was saying, gay, straight, whatever, I was about to make a ridiculously small wage for a lot of work. I've tried to forget how much time I've wasted with wages that couldn't support a ramen and dollar pizza diet. It was somewhere between nine and eleven dollars an hour if I am not mistaken.

My acting classes were during the day and it took up about 6-8 hours of my day when it was all said and done. If I had to learn lines or rehearse with a scene partner, it would tack on a few more hours. I was only able to work about 1-3 hours, a few days a week if I was lucky. If you're doing the math, this is not even a job. Luckily, my student loan covered my housing and utility costs. It came to about $1,500 per month if you broke it down per semester, but I had to pay the interest on my loan while I was attending school. It was part of my agreement. Growing up poor and never learning about finances or interest rates as a kid, I didn't know that I should have been paying more than the minimum, because Sallie Mae and all creditors wanted to rape me for as long as they could. "Sure, just pay us the interest.

How long do you want to do that before you start paying us back? Two years? No problem!"

RANT

It's literally disgusting how companies take advantage of people that have no idea about finances or how to budget. I am not blaming the people working at these companies by any means. The only reason they know about fees, interest, and principal payments are because they had to learn in order to get the desk job. Can you understand why schools don't make it mandatory to teach teenagers what to do with money before they even make it? I can't! I don't mean to go on a bit of a rant but this is some crazy shit. These are facts. Why do you think so many professional sports players blow through their millions so quickly? Look at who is teaching them what to do with their money. Look at who is teaching them to invest. It's either nobody at all or other poor people. I just feel like kids would be so much smarter than adults if we started showing them how to manage their bank accounts and finances, as soon as they knew what an allowance was.

END OF RANT

My income was so low I had to find another job. To be perfectly honest, lying is how you get the job. By just saying that you know what you're doing and that you've made the conscious decision to make your life better, they won't even notice. I was trying to be honest with all the restaurants I would walk into while asking for a job. I promise you, I must have walked into about 20-25 places requesting the dirtiest, lowest paying position in the establishment.

"Do you have experience?"

"Not yet, but I learn really fast."

"Okay. We'll be in touch."

Be in touch? I asked to clean tables and mop your floors. Fuck!

Time to cross the street and apply there, "Where have you worked in the past?"

Learning my lesson just moments earlier, I decided to try, "I used to work at a restaurant in Massachusetts, in my hometown."

This was the truth, but I was on the grill not serving tables or being a barback. I wasn't trying to lie, I just wanted to make sure it was something to say that I had some experience in that environment.

"Okay. Do you have any experience in Manhattan?"

Really, are you kidding me?

"No, Sir. I...I'm trying to gain the experience. That's why I'm here."

"Yeah...see, we're looking for individuals that have at least 3 years of experience working in the food industry. In the city."

"Okay, thank you for your time. Have a great day."

I swear I got so fucking frustrated walking in and out of these places begging for a job, for minimum wage, I snapped on one person. It wasn't like I was asking to own shares in the company or anything. I was simply asking to clean their dishes, wait tables, barback, wash and mop floors, take out the trash, whatever I had to do. One person asked me if I had any experience in the city and before she finished her sentence, I said, "No! This is why I am here. I want to gain experience, but nobody will let me. How did your other employees get their experience? If you do the math when nobody is allowing someone to gain "experience" but they only want experienced workers, how does anyone get a job? Where did they gain someone's trust? Who gave them a chance? It's ridiculous. I'll do anything."

"I don't know where they got experience but that's what we need. At least 3 years of it."

I walked out.

HOW?

Then it hit me. These people must have started lying to get the job. Why didn't I just start lying? Honesty, apparently, only gets you so far. I was raised differently.

Since I walked through Times Square and approached every restaurant there, and then I walked straight up and down 1st, 2nd, *and* 3rd avenue on the East Side begging for work in bars with no luck, I tried clothing stores.

"Do you have experience?"

"YES! A ton of it!"

"Really? Where have you worked?"

"See, right here on my resumé, it says Aldo."

I had added a shoe store near the top of my resumé because I was about to apply at a shoe store. Smart huh? Little did he know, I actually applied to Aldo back home and they had given me the job but I couldn't take it after they gave it to me. I was still being as honest as I could be.

He loved that I had experience selling shoes because

obviously, Dr. Jay's sold shoes. What a coincidence. Witnessing someone wanting to give me a job was a change of pace.

"When can you start?"

With a bit of a chuckle, "As soon as you ask!"

He said, "Great," and handed me paperwork to fill out so I could start the very next day.

At this point, I was so excited because I finally had two gigs. This job was paying a lower rate and I was about to sell shoes, but it was new to me. One of my favorite things to do is to learn. I showed up at eight o'clock in the morning, as my new boss requested. There was another kid that opened up the store about 15 minutes later than he was supposed to. Cool! It seemed like a pretty lenient place to work if you can show up late. Lenient? Woah...this place was the most boring job I've ever had. They showed me the ropes, and they showed me where the shoes were stored. I was working in the front of the building so I was greeting people when they walked in. My job was to approach them and sell them shoes, but it wasn't commission based so there was zero incentive to help these customers. Over the speakers, the playlist had the same twenty-three songs on repeat. Do you know how fast twenty-three songs, at three minutes apiece, go by? It takes just over an hour. JUST OVER AN HOUR. I heard the same song at least six times a day.

I thought, *HOLY SHIT!*

I punched out and ran out onto 34th street. I could breathe. Finally. I heard cars, people yelling, brakes screeching, horns blasting, and the echo of sirens reflecting off the skyscrapers.

Thank God! I'm FREE!

I walked to the New Yorker hotel to see my girlfriend at the time and she asked how it went. I told her I didn't want to go back the next day.

"Isaac, you need this. Try again!"

"But, I hate it! I can't!"

"You haven't been able to find a job and now you have one. It's going to allow to pay for your loan." She pleaded with me.

"You're right. Maybe it was just a slow day. I'll try again tomorrow." I couldn't believe the words came out of my mouth.

I started on a Saturday. Sunday, I was scheduled to work again. Same time, same place, same shit, different day. Luckily, the day before the kid that opened up for us was a nice guy and we got along. We weren't best friends but he was nice. He showed me the ins and outs of the place and we were forced to stand next to each other all day the day before. When there was one customer every fifteen minutes that walked through, we had to do something. All the shoes can only be organized and neatly placed on plexiglass shelves so many times. He opened the doors for day number two and began "working" before he went over to the sound system and pressed play.

Here we go again! I thought.

Lunch rolls around and my girlfriend thought it would be a lovely idea to swing by and brighten up my day. It was. What a relief it was to see someone I loved in what felt like the most depressing place on the planet. There were no customers, so the only things to do were to think and listen to music. The same music. Every hour. I am not exaggerating, I felt like a zombie. It was so good to see her. I have a very vivid memory of her face popping around the glass windows as she stood outside inviting me to go out and talk to her. I walked out and kissed her and said, "What am I doing?"

I wanted to cry, felt so out of place, and I knew in my heart I was so much better than this.

"Are you okay?" She asked.

"I'm going to leave! TODAY!"

She didn't know how to reply because she could see my mind had been made up for hours. She kissed me goodbye and wished me luck. She also supported the decision because she didn't have a choice.

At the end of the day, I found the owner and told him I was leaving. I even remember him getting really pissed off when I told him. From his point of view, it must have been obnoxious because he had to submit paperwork for my check and he took a risk hiring me. I told him I didn't even care if he paid me. The funny thing was (I had never seen a company do this until now) but when I clocked in I had to use my fingerprint and because it was so high tech and advanced, he didn't have a choice but to pay me. I got to say, that felt pretty awesome. Stickin' it to "The Man" in my own sort of way. My check was about sixty dollars and I had to go back and pick it up 10 days later or something like that. It was awkward as fuck when I walked back in and saw the guys I was just working with. They looked miserable and I had accomplished something they had yet to attempt: I got out. You could see it on their faces. It was insane.

My former boss had some wise-ass thing to say for me to ponder upon my escape as if it mattered that he was pissed off. I couldn't have given a flying fuck, to be honest. I was free and that was by far the most dream killing experience of my entire life. I feel like being a robot would have been more entertaining. Literally, you try standing in a two-foot by two-foot area, on "your side" of the store, with a speaker replaying the same song over and over again and not go insane? I DID IT! I was free. For now.

Now, once again, job hunting became a priority. This time around I knew one thing I did not want to do, so that was a plus. Also, I knew that I had to lie to get what I wanted. My girlfriend and I walked around on 34th street again to see where I should work next. I don't know if she just enjoyed window shopping or really supported my search for a job. No, she was always very supportive when it came to me working.

We came across this crazy looking store called Desigual. It's Spanish for "Not The Same." Their clothing line was definitely not the same as any other clothing store on 34th street. In fact, the only other store that looked similar was their own store a few blocks away. They were and still are a very unique store.

I love art, colors, and creativity. Where better to work than here? Sweet!

I applied and a few days later, I got a phone call for an interview. I was so stoked. Interviews are my shit. They don't scare me whatsoever. My interview was scheduled after my theatre job one night. What was great about this new job was that it was literally about a ten-minute walk from my current position at the Academy. It just felt right before I even had my interview. There are moments in life where you just know what the end result will be, and this was one of those moments. It was so close to my daily route already, it just made sense. I walked in.

The manager sits me down and she comes at me with, "Do you have experience in retail?"

I replied, "Yes! See? Right here, I...I've worked at Aldo and...ah...Dr. Jays."

The shoe store job was literally a couple of stores down on

the same block and she couldn't believe it, "The one down the street?"

"Yup! That's the one."

"Why did you leave?"

"I didn't! I still work there. I'm just looking for extra hours."

She said, "Oh, okay, perfect. Can you start this weekend?"

"Absolutely!"

SUCKER!!

After I got the job, I ended up telling my manager, after I had worked my ass off and we were close enough to have a laugh, that I had lied on my resumé and she laughed at me.

She said, "Isaac, I found that out pretty quickly when you didn't know what 'inventory' was."

We laughed wicked hard and she then proceeded to compliment my drive and willingness to learn even though she knew my secret. This job was probably one of my favorite jobs in the city. I know that sounds weird but I loved talking to people and because the store was so unique, people would flood the store. On occasion I'd be bored out my mind but only if I had to mindlessly fold clothes or space the racks. Spacing the racks meant that you had to make sure each coat hanger was a finger's width apart. It looked really pretty when they were all done but then a customer would come over and fuck up your hard work and there was never a point where you felt like you accomplished anything. The only time you felt proud of your hard work was when you closed the store and opened the next morning when everything was left exactly how you left it the night before. Of course, sometimes *that* didn't even happen because the cleaners would bump shit or move around your displays after you left.

Once and a while, I would be asked to hand out a bunch of our little catalogs that had examples of everything in the store. I would also hand out bags to try to get people to fill them up inside our store. It was clever, but I was scared at first. They would just throw me in front of the store, right on the sidewalk and tell me, "Go get us some traffic!"

It's easier said than done, but man, I became a pro. I learned to love that position. At one point they gave me a headset with a speaker attached to it. It was dope, I was louder now. You could hear my Dad Jokes on the other side of 34th street now. The real reason I loved that job was the sheer number of gorgeous women just walking by me. Never saying "Hi," never catcalling, just admiring the exceptional qualities of these luscious individuals.

Women are fucking hilarious. As a man, I walk down the street and if I think I see something I'm attracted to, I keep looking. It's important not to stare but to look with high hopes of reciprocation in my direction. Sometimes, it's what a British friend of mine calls a "M.A.P., Modern Art Piece," and sometimes, it's exactly what I thought I saw or even better as she approached me. It's called M.A.P. because a lot of modern art looks beautiful from far away and then close up, it's basic as fuck. You can use it for men as well. It's just someone that you found super attractive and then you felt deceived as your vision cleared up. I love the phrase.

Women, however, are so much more subtle about it. I swear they notice a man from about a mile away and they won't even acknowledge the fact that you're looking at them. They know you're looking at them and they may or may not love it. If they do, they don't want you to know they were looking as well. So they wait until they're just about to pass you. As your shoulder and their shoulder are at about ten o'clock, she will swing both of her eyes ninety degrees in your direction. It's accompanied by a slight smirk, just enough to confirm she knew what she was talking about from a mile away.

If you aren't careful, if you aren't watching closely, you would never know they even looked your way. I am speaking from experience here. This had happened to me almost every day in NYC. Nothing happens after that moment but the rush you feel when it does is incredible. It's as if someone injected a turbo shot from Dunkins' straight to your heart. Without the pain of the needle, obviously. I can't tell you how many times it's happened and when it does, you feel like a Greek God.

You would also enjoy that job. It was basically getting paid to flirt and attract customers to your store.

Piece of cake!

My next favorite job at this place was the dressing room. It was a unisex dressing room and people would try on so many different combinations of outfits, it was quite interesting to watch. That wasn't my favorite bit, though. It was the fact that I got to be honest with the customer and give them real feedback on what they were about to purchase. They respected my opinion so much. I wasn't trying to sell them on whatever they tried on and lie to their face. I was different. Again, I am a fan of honesty.

Men would ask, "Does this look too tight?"

I would say, "Yes, maybe try a size bigger."

If the colors didn't compliment their complexion and features, I would tell them to try another color. Women, would walk out half naked and ask for help with strings, buttons, ties, you name it. Even shit that wasn't our clothing. I would help women put their own clothes back on.

It was just a very interesting time and it always went by so fast. I got to meet so many people from all around the world. The majority of the customers were foreign and just passing through as they traveled the United States. There were so many different cultures and stories in that one tiny, mirrored, room. It got to the point where I knew where all the clothing was and what sizes we had left. When I could run out to the floor and grab a dress or a pair of pants and run back with what the customer wanted in less than a minute, it was rewarding. They would usually buy something because they could see I was ready to take care of them. I learned a lot about working with customers, one on one, in Desigual.

Don't get me wrong, there were some wicked pain in the ass customers. One older, bougie, woman walked in and asked us to turn the music down. Another asked us to turn off the air conditioning.

What? Why would you even think we would cater to only your needs and forget about the other twenty customers here?

Of course, I never said that to her face. It's a ridiculous assumption. I never understood how people would think they were better than someone else and that their shopping experience mattered more.

One of our customers really enjoyed his shopping experience. We had a security guard at the front of the store and he would walk around and double check the racks or customers and watch their movements. He would warn us, in code, if he suspected someone was popping off the sensors or switching price tags. It was about seven o'clock one evening, and I had just got off a break. I went to the front of the store and the security guard had walked to the back.

The break room had a staircase in it because it wasn't a break room originally, it was an exit with lockers in it. Under the stairs, there was an opening with coats and bags or returns and things of that nature. The security guard walked in and grabbed something and walked back to the front of the store. I started to have a conversation with him when he returned, but then I realized I had to check my phone and headed back to the lockers. I opened the locker and my phone was gone. My wallet was gone. All my personal shit was gone. In a frenzy, I ran out to the manager and told her about what happened. I told her what I was missing and she played back the security cameras as fast as she could.

There was a little room adjacent to the break room that housed all the kid's clothing and to the right of it, was the entrance to the break room. Which was was so inconspicuous that it took me a while to remember where it was when I first started. There was a camera in the kid's room and one in the break room. As we rewound the camera footage of the break room, we saw that *I* was looking for my shit and freaking out. Just before that, we saw the security guard go grab something out of his locker. We kept rewinding to the entry of the guard. Still nothing unusual. As we switched cameras, we started to rewind the kid's room footage. We went back further and saw a man in a hoodie, open up the door, and let himself into the break room. He was not an employee and he had a hood on. We switched back to the break room camera and matched up the times. Sure enough, this little fucker opened all the lockers and took whatever he pleased.

Now, the question that was still on our mind was, "Where was he when the guard walked in?"

Again, we matched the times from both cameras and just before the guard walked in, the thief heard the door and tucked himself under the staircase. After security left, the robber popped out and just walked out of the break room. Nobody was expecting anything, so he was able to walk right by both of us at the front of the store. Out the door, he went.

I couldn't believe it. I had literally just freed myself from a phone plan that had contracts. Silly me decided to buy a phone outright from Walmart and use Straight Talk. It was a cheap phone bill but the phone itself was a flip phone with a full keyboard and it cost me a couple of hundred dollars. At the time, a couple of hundred bucks was two weeks pay for me. It was heartbreaking. Because I bought the phone outright and it was prepaid, there was no insurance plan that came with it. I tried to go cheap and it would have been cheaper for me to just pay the deductible from the contracted phone plan in the end. Live and learn, right?

Of course, my wallet had my MetroCard in it and at the time, I lived between East 96th and 97th on Lexington Avenue. Desigual was on East 34th and Madison. I didn't have money for a cab because my wallet was stolen and I couldn't ride the subway because my card was stolen. It was a brand new 30-Day Unlimited MetroCard as well. If you are from NYC, you know just how deep that dagger pierced.

We called the police and they filled out a report. There was absolutely no way to tell who this man was or what he looked like. The cameras were trash and the hoodie looked really comfortable with a massive hood that covered his entire face. I told the police what had happened and that I was missing all my belongings. I needed to get home and I really didn't want to walk sixty-three blocks and a few avenues to get home at eleven at night. They totally understood and gave me a slip that said I had two free MTA rides. How awesome was that?

After this happened, I ended up having to order a new license, phone and bought myself a new MetroCard. Sometimes you have zero control over what happens to you and I suggest that you roll with the punches and keep moving forward.

That incident, and having to rearrange the store at two o'clock in the morning every few months, were the worst days of that job. Everything else was smooth sailing from there. A position in the job that I really enjoyed was working the cash register. I learned about credit card transactions and inventory. We had a system in place to check inventory so we knew when to order more or what items were returned to the store. I learned a lot. For instance, I had no idea that some clothing companies used pieces of clothing from a few seasons ago and marketed it as clearance or sale. I know this sounds obvious but sometimes they would literally just take a shirt from four years ago, hang it up and say clearance. It makes sense because you want to sell as many pieces as you can. The other thing they did was use the same "design or style," several years in a row. The only difference was color and maybe a pattern adjustment based on customer feedback. They weren't producing new pieces every day. They were testing. It was a wake-up call for me when I realized how easy it was to keep issuing "new" products on the floor.

One time, I had to check the inventory to make sure we received the correct number of items that they had ordered. Sometimes we would be missing a few pieces or buttons and zippers would fall off during shipping. While double checking our order, I came across a price next to each item. I will not disclose the exact amount but when I saw how dirt cheap these tee shirts cost, I was shocked. For example, we would sell tee shirts for sixty dollars plus, in our store and the tee shirt would cost the company, let's say two to five bucks each. I'm talking fifty-five dollars profit. If I remember correctly, this was with shipping included.

I was like, *What the fuck am I reading?*

It blew my mind, *This is how retail works?*

Even then, I hadn't fully grasped the difference between wholesale and retail pricing. I was just touching the surface and at the same time widening my vision.

It made me think, *Hmmm, why can't I do this? Buy low and sell high.*

9

THE PURPLE TASSELED HELICOPTER

Y ou are probably thinking, *What did I just read?*

Let me explain: At this time, I had two jobs. I was working for AADA, right after school, and I was working for Desigual after AADA, but because these jobs were paying minimum wage I still needed more money. Decisions had to be made.

There were a few male strip clubs in Manhattan that I could apply to. I was about a hundred and fifty pounds with eight percent body fat. I had been modeling and shooting photos for many years prior to moving to New York City. It wasn't unusual for me to be naked or to imply that I was naked while I was on set in front of multiple people and I'm very confident with who I am.

I figured, *Why not,* and I sent an email to three clubs that looked nice and the reviews were really good. Attached to the email were a few shirtless photos and a headshot, as you do. A few minutes later, I received a reply from one of them.

I thought, *That was fast. Maybe they have an automatic reply set up for submissions.*

Nope. It was the manager of the club. He requested that I swing down to Times Square and meet with him when I was available.

It just so happened that I was not scheduled to work that evening and I had some free time, so I replied and told him I would be down in forty minutes.

Here we go!

I was about to walk into a world that I had never set foot in before that day. Until that point, I had never even been into a strip club, let alone a male strip club. I was a little scared at the same time. The first thing that crossed my mind was, *What did I just get myself into?*

Forty minutes later, I arrived and had to walk into a building that appeared to be closed or out of business. The only reason I thought they could be open was that the metal garage style door was open three-quarters of the way. It was high enough where I didn't have to duck but it looked like I shouldn't go in. So I did. (After all, I am only 5'8" and sometimes I add half an inch just for fun.) I walked down the staircase and entered a dimly light room with glitter and fake crystal on the walls. It was so gaudy looking. When it came time for them to turn the lights off, I assumed you wouldn't notice the alcohol stained floor tiles. The chairs were the black metal folder chairs. The ones you would use as back up if the nice chairs were all taken.

This should be interesting! I thought.

Across the room, there was a man summoning me to walk over to his side of the room. He was definitely not going to approach me. It was clear that *I* was in *his* territory. His arms were massive. He was fully clothed, wearing a button-down, long sleeve shirt. His hair was done to perfection. Even though he was fully clothed, I could tell he lived at the gym. Eating healthy and working out was exactly what his idea of a good time was. He introduced himself and I could barely understand him. He had a really strong accent which I believe was Russian. I'm not quite sure because I was too afraid to ask. He was so fucking intimidating.

Out of the corner my eye, there were a couple more foreign-looking men. They had to be at least six feet tall...while sitting. Seriously, these guys were giants in every way. I walked in around a hundred and fifty pounds, eight percent body fat, and 5'8." They all had to be at least 6'5", zero percent body fat, and a minimum of two hundred and twenty pounds of solid muscle. I was so out of place it was hilarious. The assumed Russian man in front of me introduced himself again when I didn't understand him the first time. Slowly but surely, my ears started to decipher his accent, "You are, Isaac?"

"Yes!" I replied in a voice that barely made it out of vocal cords.

"Do you have experience, Isaac?"

Here we go again.

"In what field?" I said.

"Dancing, Isaac." Looking at me like I was a complete moron.

I kept thinking, *Why does he keep saying my name? I'm already intimidated. STOP!*

I managed to be truthful and not lie, "No. Um, I would...I would love to learn though."

"Okay, that is fine. We teach you. Do you at least have experience waiting tables?"

FUCK! Not again...Say something, Isaac!

"YES!"

"You do? Excellent! You will take order and serve the women drinks."

Wait a minute! Did he just give me a job?

Enthusiastically, I said, "Okay. I can definitely do that."

He looked into my soul with his expressionless face. This is when I knew I did not have the job as of yet.

"Take your shirt off!"

"Okay?" I was a little confused but understood why.

"Walk over there and walk back towards me."

"Okay." I felt like a piece of meat, but *Okay!*

"Isaac, you can work tonight?"

Instantly, I thought, *Fuck, my girlfriend is going to be so mad when I tell her I need to postpone dinner this evening.*

I had no idea I was going to be working that night and because I didn't have work, I wanted to spend time with my lady. Pretty logical thought.

That thought lasted about point two seconds and I replied without hesitation, "Yes!"

"Good. See her? She will take care of you."

I think it might have been his girlfriend or something.

I said, "Thank you," as I walked over to the woman.

She said, "You can put your shirt back on. Next time, wear black shoes and black pants. Tonight, you are okay. I need your license. I need to scan."

I said, "Why?"

"Because it's for safety reasons. You may go by a code name

or you may steal and this is not on books. You are dancing for tips only. There is no paycheck. We just want to be safe with customers."

It made sense in my head. I pulled out my wallet and gave her my license. She came back with a photocopy of my license and just wanted me to sign it. She also asked what size shirt I was.

"Medium," I said.

She left me standing there and returned with a gray tank top. There was a bodybuilder on the front of the tank and it looked pretty cool. That was it. I got the job and I had a "uniform." It was a little confusing because I thought I would have no shirt on but then I realized that I was just starting out and I didn't even come close to the other guy's when we would be standing side by side.

I thought, *I'll keep this on!*

My confidence level went right out the door.

There was a bit of time to kill before the women started showing up. They said it would be a slow evening. I had no idea what I was doing, so slow was good. I was introduced to a few dancers and they seemed really nice. To be honest, these guys were awesome. I went into the back room which was the changing room or green room for all the performers. I placed my bag down and found a spot out of the way.

"Hi." I nervously said to a couple of guys and they made me feel right at home.

They spoke English but looked like they were straight out of an Italian Men's Fashion Magazine. They probably were. It was crazy. I have never felt more unattractive in my life. It was humbling, to say the least. They started to show me the ropes and talk to me about what to expect while they were all eating chicken and rice. These dudes were telling stories of the women from nights in the past and how crazy they were. I was about to find out for myself.

I took a moment to call my girlfriend and inform her that her boyfriend just landed a gig at a strip club but I wasn't stripping. I wasn't even dancing yet. They had told me that I would get to rehearse with them tomorrow if I decided to show up. There was no schedule. The assumption was that you would show up and if you didn't show for a certain number of nights, you don't dance there anymore. It was simple.

My girlfriend just laughed and said, "Have fun."

She was supportive in a "Don't tell me about all the women that will want to fuck you," kind of way. It was funny. I felt bad, but I needed the money. I definitely didn't want grandma killing me.

After my phone call and before the doors opened, one of the guys took me to grab a slice of pizza across the street. He was just giving me more details on what to expect and what not.

We headed back over to the club and he said, "Before they come, I usually have a shot or two to loosen up. You want one?"

I said, "Sure."

"Cool. Yeah, these women come in here and they're scared because they don't know how to react or they're shy. Sometimes they just want to look and have nothing to say. Sometimes they'll be too afraid to ask for what they really want. If you are uncomfortable, they'll sense that and that's just bad business for both of us. So, loosen up. Be confident. They'll feed off of that."

I was interested in seeing how these women reacted. I am a firm believer in taking on new experiences. This is one that I will never forget. I took a shot and it hit me quick. I had to piss real quick before the women got there and I knew the door would be opening any minute. I ran to the bathroom and made sure to freshen up. They had mints and stuff in the bathroom. After washing my hands, I turned around to exit and noticed an enormous box on the wall that said "Condoms." I didn't know what to think about that as I had never seen condoms in a public bathroom. The best part is, it said they were issued by New York City itself. Better safe than sorry. I thought that was genius.

The doors opened and I started to see women make their way to the uncomfortable black metal seats that we set up around the tables. The rows were so tight it was hard not to accidentally fall into women's laps while you were walking around. I just sat back and absorbed as much as I could about how this whole thing worked. It was more of a learning experience that I got to participate in at the same time. Since these women were so nervous, the first guy that came over to talk to them would most likely be the one they were most comfortable with for the remainder of the night. This caused a little drama between the performers because some guys would just rush over to the table as soon as the women sat down and it ended up being the classic, "You snooze, you lose," situation. I learned pretty quickly to keep my eyes on the door and tried to guess which table they were walking to. I also learned how to estimate the amount they were willing to spend that evening.

I started walking over to the women and asking if it was their first time at the venue and tried to make them feel as comfortable as possible. My next job was to take their drink orders and hit up the bartender. Of course, the bartender took a percentage at the end of each night. It wasn't anything crazy but one night, I remember only being able to make seventeen dollars for a four-hour shift. Since I wasn't a dancer, I was only making money off of tips and the women would tip the dancers and performers way more than the drink dude, obviously.

It wasn't going according to plan and some nights I would make forty dollars over four hours. This was not enough money for me to live off of either so I wanted to start dancing. The guys had a routine that changed every few weekends. The show would open up with the host and then a dancer would perform a solo dance for the women. It would vary. There were a few group dances as well and it was my turn to learn the group dance. They were teaching me but very quickly. I had to really learn fast because I only had about thirty minutes to practice each night with the guys. The dance was five minutes long. Looking back, they kept me in the back for good reasons. I didn't know what the fuck I was doing and I'm not a dancer. Not even close. I'm blatantly English.

As I was learning how to dance with the group, I got singled out as the new guy and was asked to just go up on stage and give it my best shot to perform a solo act. This was probably the most embarrassing moment of my entire life. I am not camera shy nor do I get stage fright. When it came to dancing for men to tell me whether or not I could dance for women, it was a game changer. I froze.

I couldn't help but think, *I don't want to act all sexy and try to turn on other men.*

It was really difficult to get over. I didn't have a choice because this was the only way I would make a decent amount of cash every night. I remember standing up there and the spotlight was blasting on my face but it wasn't bright enough to blur out all the other six foot, two hundred and twenty pound, Italian imports glaring at me. It was not my best moment. I moved a little left, a little right, a little up and down and around and it felt so weird. I definitely failed that one. The boss didn't even let me finish whatever it was I tried to start.

"Okay, Isaac. Thanks."

Fuck my life!

Needless to say, it was back to serving shots in plastic cups. It wasn't all bad, some of the women were stunning and I got to chat them up and because I was working there, it automatically made me sexier in their eyes. It was awesome. Some women acted as if they had never seen a six pack or a man's chest in their entire life. They were insane. Even sober, they just acted like whatever they said or did was never going to be said or done again in their life, so "Fuck it!"

I had one girl bend me over backward, pulled the front of my underwear with her left hand and with her right, she successfully rolled a dollar coin along the center of my stomach and into my underwear. It was insane. She did it several times. The dollar coins were so cold. That's all I remember, the metal just sitting there under my boys. I remember taking them out in the bathroom and putting them in my pocket.

Coins? Who goes to a strip club with coins? It was a laugh, to say the least.

This is the best part of working there and unfortunately the most vivid memory I have of the establishment. There was, again, a six-foot giant. He looked like a Greek God with no fat on him. He had been working at this place for years and he was so confident, unlike this newbie. He wore a purple tasseled thong. THAT WAS IT. In NYC, apparently, men are not allowed to show their genitals. (Did you know that? I had no idea but thanks to the gods that was the case.) One night, a couple of cackling hens rolled up and sat in the front of the room. It was one of the ladies' bachelorette parties. It was her last night as a "free" woman so she went to town. She got called up to the stage because her friends were really instigating.

It was usual for the birthday girls and brides to get special dances performed just for them if they paid enough. Her friends paid enough to get her a dance up on stage. Her role consisted of sitting in a chair. That's all she had to do. THAT'S IT! Sounds pretty easy and harmless right? She was so fucking kinky. The big dude comes out, looking like Vin Diesel, wearing his famous little thong that looked like it had to be customized specifically for his dick. I swear, I have never seen anything so big in my life. Imagine a small wooden bat bent down to the ground due to its gravitational pull. Have you got that image in your head? Okay, good. Now imagine the backdrop for your senior prom, all glittery and shiny. Now imagine those tassels taped to the wooden bat as it bends, searching for the floor. I swear this thing was huge. Realistically, *I* felt like a female after seeing the size of *his*. Should I keep going? No? You get it? Okay. Sorry.

Alright, so she is sitting on the chair and somehow ends up on the floor of the stage, on her back. He spins her over and dances all around her. She managed to get to her knees while feeling as if she was in heaven or something. She was smiling, laughing, drunk, horny, begging, and whatever else she was doing. While on her knees, she yells out, "HIT ME WITH IT!"

He stops and just laughs. It caught him off guard. *He* could barely make out what she had said because the music was so loud and *he* was wearing the only mic on stage. *We* all heard her though. He turns to the crowd as he helicopters his dong around, just missing her face. He says, "This bitch is crazy!"

Proceeding to turn around and contemplating whether or not he should abuse her with his bat, the crowd is in stitches, laughing at how unreal this experience is.

We hear her scream again, "I said, HIT ME WITH IT!"

He walks up to her, dong in face, as if *she* was about to please *him*. Although the roles were about to be reversed. He lifts it up and just drops it on her forehead. I couldn't believe what I was witnessing. It was probably the funniest thing I had ever seen. You couldn't help but laugh and watch to see what else she wanted him to try. Fortunately, that was all he was allowed to do. She went a little crazy after that, almost started to cry with joy.

It's a very peculiar feeling when you are a guy and women are trying to grab your penis or ass cheeks and begging for more. It's usually the men chasing the women but not here. This was totally different. I had never experienced women acting like this. I actually had to turn down numbers because I had a girlfriend at the time. I felt bad.

If you ever get the chance to witness something like this for yourself, it makes a great story and it just goes to show you that you only understand what you are surrounded by. There is more to life. There are so many different cultures and ways of living. At first, we don't know they exist. Then we learn about them and judge them because we don't understand it fully. There is no right or wrong in situations like that, just new experiences. Who am I to judge the girl on stage for just letting loose? Who am I to judge the guy that made her cry with happiness? It was just unreal.

10

SLOW SUMMERS

S ummers were slow at the Academy and as I said before, because the dancing gig wasn't paying enough, I ended up having to quit that job too. Since dancing was my third job, I just asked for more hours on the weekends at my second job, the retail store, and somehow made that work. For quite some time, I worked at the retail store and AADA on a daily basis. AADA was slow during the summer. Since it's a school, there were no sets to build for plays or performances when the students were gone on vacation. It allowed me to work even more hours at the retail store. My boss at AADA (we'll call him Joe) would take Fridays off and leave early on Thursdays sometimes, so I would just fuck off on Fridays.

He can leave early and take time off. Why can't I?!

It makes complete sense right? Hear the entrepreneurial side popping through there? He was nice enough to get to know me to the point where he knew I had bills to pay and he wasn't paying nearly enough to support my cost of living. He recommended me to a guy that used to work in the same exact position that I was in, who now owned his own woodworking company. Let me tell you, this new guy was about to change my life.

One day, Joe sent me to Brooklyn to meet this new guy. Apparently, he had some work that I could do. It was a long ass trip from the Upper East Side but I needed the money badly. I was told to show up around seven o'clock in the morning. (In NYC, I don't remember if I mentioned this before but, places don't open until at least eight. I couldn't even get a coffee before I arrived.) That being said, I arrived on time. I was all ready to work a long laborious day. It was in Gowanus, Brooklyn, which was all shops, factories, and warehouses. At the time, that is. It changed in just a short period of time. Anyways, I couldn't find the entrance and the garage door was shut. I was knocking and nobody was answering. I could see through the glass in the garage door and out of the darkness comes this dude wearing black jeans and a plaid, long sleeve, shirt. That is the only outfit he ever wore. Obviously, it would change but that was his style. He seemed really cool and he didn't look much older than I was.

I thought, *How does this guy own his own business? He's young.*

He opened the garage door and said, "I told Joe to send me some fucking muscle, not a twink!"

If you don't know what a twink is, it's a tiny, hairless, gay man. I only knew that because of modeling back in the day and it was thrown around in the industry a little bit.

We both busted out laughing and he said, "I'm Chris, nice to meet you."

His name really isn't Chris, but just for the sake of this story, it is now.

I said, "I'm Isaac. Nice to meet you."

"Sorry, Joe and I go way back. I knew if you were working with him, you were able to take a joke."

To this day, I have never met anyone that started a conversation with such a solid joke that actually could offend me but not offend me at the same time. He got me good. After all this knocking and getting made fun of, it was time to get to work.

"Alright, so I can give you twenty dollars an hour but I need you to sit here and wait for a delivery. Okay?"

I thought to myself, *Is he fucking serious? This is the most money I ever have made per hour in my life and it's cash.*

Cool, calm, and collected, I said, "Yeah, no problem. When's the delivery supposed to be here?"

"A couple hours."

"Okay, I can do that."

"I may have some more work for you when I get back, cool?"

"Yup!"

At least forty to sixty dollars was about to be placed in my pocket. That was equivalent to four to six hours of work usually. It was literally double my pay and cash. Chris left and I just sat in a chair with the garage door open, waiting for something to be delivered. I didn't even know what it was, but there I was, making the most money I had ever made per hour. Did that mean I couldn't go backward now?

Is my worth at least twenty bucks an hour now?

I was excited. I stuck my headphones in and just listened to some tunes on my iPod. Since NYC doesn't open until about eight a.m, nobody was even walking by the shop and nobody else was at this shop yet.

I could tell there were other offices and different companies all in this one building. It was kind of cool. I hadn't seen anything like this. There were logos and branding everywhere, it wasn't just one business. There was a workshop at the back of the building that housed a few work-benches and a couple of machines for woodwork. There were a few storage racks and not many tools. Tools were kept in the little "offices" on a cart and they would be rolled to the workshop as needed. Each "office" was surrounded by at least three walls made of two by fours and plywood. Some had been painted and others were not. Essentially, it was a shared workspace and everyone had locks to their "offices" that looked more like small storage units. The inside of the offices were all different depending on what the artist did for a living. There was a metal shop in the back as well. Some people were painters, builders, welders, and printers and so on. It was nice to see a variety of trades housed in one facility. Before that, I didn't even know that was a thing.

After I snooped around a little bit, I got bored of not being able to see into other offices, so I decided to sit and wait. The delivery arrived carrying wood. If I am not mistaken, they were beautiful walnut boards. They were hand selected by Chris and they looked gorgeous if you like that sort of thing. No knots, just perfect grain patterns. Don't get me started.

The only reason I remember this was because it couldn't have been more than a few days later when I royally fucked up the hand selected boards. Chris told me to go grab a Forstner bit so I could drill some holes. Around the corner from the shop was a Lowes or as we liked to call it "Slows" because the customer service in that Lowes location is horrendous.

Jumping ahead here, there was a day that my coworker and I went to go grab some materials and there was a guy yelling in the isles, at the top of his lungs. He was screaming, "Help me! Help Me! I need help, Please, someone help me!"

We tried to find where it was coming from because we wanted to help.

Then we heard, "Can I get some fucking help here? Jesus! Is anyone working here? Hello? Fuck, I hate this place!"

It was hilarious. This dude clearly knew that the only way to get the employees attention was to pretend to be injured. The funniest bit was they never even came over to him. What? We were laughing so hard and it became an inside joke.

HELP ME!

Anyways, back to Chris. He asked me to grab a bit to drill some holes. Easy enough, right? Wrong!

I thought, *I know what I am doing! I got this!*

I was a little bit too cocky this time around. I had my bits mixed up in my head so I bought a bit, that drilled the same size hole in diameter *but* it was for drilling rough holes that could be an estimated size. I grabbed a *paddle* bit instead of a *Forstner* bit. One drills perfectly beautiful holes and just pokes through the wood so you don't end up blowing out the back of the board. (That would be the Forstner bit.) However, the paddle bit only has two blades, or edges, to bore a hole. Thus, causing wood chips to go everywhere. The center of the bit has a long sharp point that will penetrate through the face of the other side long before the "paddles" even touch the face of the opposite side. Depending on the thickness of the wood. Because of this, the point will go first, to start the hole and burst through the board and the paddles will basically smash around, in a rotating fashion, following the point until it breaks through the other side. With a Forstner bit, the point is small so you can flip the board over and if you have gone slow enough through the face on the other side, the point will have *just* popped a small hole in the back side. From there, you're able to start drilling from the back and lightly pop through to the other side to finish the hole. By doing this, you'll have a perfectly smooth hole with no broken edges or splinters on either side. Just wood shavings and a clean hole. The paddle bit is a wild beast.

I'm sure I just lost you but what happened was, I used the wrong bit and the hole ended up wider than it should have been due to the uncontrollable paddles that whipped around. That was the first mistake. The second was that once I started drilling the first hole into the face of the wood, it was too late. I tried to stop before I got all the way through the board, but it burst right through anyway. Mind, you, these pieces were already cut and milled to size. This was one of the finishing touches and we needed these holes to be very, very precise to fit a light fixture that was going to be attached to it. It almost had to be snug with *some* wiggle room for humidity. This being said, I destroyed the face of the beautiful walnut piece and he wasn't there for me to show him what happened. I thought if I went slower, next time, it wouldn't happen. That just wasn't the case. The same thing happened, if not worse. See, I knew it looked like shit but I figured I could sand it, smooth out the edges of the hole and get away with it. Guess what happened there?

At this time, I was only told to grab the bit and drill the holes. I had no idea what they were being used for until after I had fucked them up. In fairness, not that I didn't royally mess these boards up, but if I was told beforehand what these were used for and how we were going to assemble them, I wouldn't have tried to fix my mistake. However, because I attempted to repair this issue by sanding it, the hole expanded. And when we went to place the wooden piece around the light fixture, there was a quarter inch gap, all the way around. Nothing was hidden and what was meant to look like a circular hole, now looked like an oval after sanding the shit out of it.

Chris got back and got really pissed off. As a small business owner, or for any business for that matter, these mistakes cost the company, not the customer. I didn't give a shit about "the company" while I was working in a massive shop or with a school that got funding from the state.

Who cares? Just go buy more materials. I thought.

That mentality got me into a lot of trouble while I worked for small furniture businesses. This is why I take so much time to prepare for a project nowadays. I need to understand and figure out as much I can before starting so there are fewer hiccups along the way and less money out of my pocket.

∼

It was only right that he made me pay for the mistake. He literally made me pay for my own mistake. As in, I wasn't getting paid a penny until this mistake was paid for out of my own wage. It taught me a massive lesson. Here it is:

If, for whatever reason, you are unsure about something or you just don't remember the specifics, just ask questions.

I can't tell you how important this information is. It will cost both you and your employer or employee so much money in addition to the endless number of headaches when the information regarding a job is not understood in its entirety. Please let my mistake be a lesson for you before you have to go through it yourself. From that day on, I was very cautious about working with him. I had to listen to every detail and ask as many questions as I needed if I wasn't able to grasp what the outcome was supposed to be. Sometimes even the process of something would conflict with what I had learned in school and I had to refresh my memory with new trade secrets. Here is another lesson:

Because I asked so many questions, I learned so much faster.

Even if I thought I already knew the answer, I would ask again. This allowed me to get paid a wage that I was happy making at the time and it was the highest paying gig for me back then. He knew I wanted to learn and the more info he gave me, the more tasks he could pass off to me. With my old way of thinking, the more I learned, the more I would know, the more jobs I would be asked to participate in, meaning more hours. More hours equaled more income. This is not the way you should do math but that was my "poor" mindset. I am not rich yet. YET! However, my "Rich" mentality has a new outlook.

Work less. Make more money.

Sounds ridiculous, right? I hope by the end of this book, you also see money the way I see money. It all starts with how much you value yourself. I'll use myself as an example.

If I say, "I am so valuable. I am worth $20 per hour."

Guess what? I will end up finding gigs that pay in that price range.

Someone's going to say, "Hey, Isaac. Listen, I've got a gig and I can pay $15/hour this week. Do you want it?"

I would have to think about it and convince myself that it's worth it, "It's only $5 per hour lower. It's close enough. At least I have the work."

If you do the math here, you'll find that I wanted $800 at the end of a 40 hour work week and now I only have $600. I just lost $200. That sucks, right? Now let's do it the opposite way.

I get told, "Isaac, I have a gig that pays $25 per hour for this week. Do you want it?"

I take the job and work 40 hours. This week I made $1,000.

"Woah! That's awesome."

Okay, chill out! If I think I am worth $20 per hour but I lowered my value to $15 per hour the week before, I need to subtract the loss of $200 from the $1,000. I end up at $800 again which is what I valued myself at, to begin with. See where I am going with this? For a moment, I thought I was ballin' because I was getting paid more than I valued myself but because I worked for less than my value the week before, it evens out. See how I ended up making the exact amount I valued myself at?

I don't know if I am explaining this well enough but if you want to work for yourself (which is the only way to make the kind of money you really want in life) then you need to understand this. If someone is coming to you for help, it is your duty to stand up for yourself and negotiate the wage. If they can't pay what you know you are worth, fuck them! I mean it. I have found myself trapped in so many situations where I took a low paying gig and I was doing astronomical amounts of work and it felt like I should have been making way more money. Who's fault is that? Not my employers, that's for damn sure. It's mine, for accepting the low wage.

The person coming to *YOU* for *YOUR* skill set wants to hire *YOU*. Who do you think should create the rate? BINGO. *YOU!* Are you catching on? Don't let them act like they're doing *YOU* a favor. They're the ones that are practically begging for *YOUR* assistance by a mutual exchange of currency to pay *YOUR* bills. Why would *YOU* let someone else determine whether or not *YOUR* bills are paid on time? I don't get it. It's a fucking insult, to be quite frank.

❦

Let's do this. I'm jumping *way* ahead here, to present day, but the other day, I was able to acquire a booth at an expo to showcase my video production skills. I learned so much from this experience. I shot a little one minute video for my barber in exchange for a haircut. It was nothing too crazy.

In my mind, I thought, *"THIS, is worth $250, easily."*

Notice how I said "THIS?"

That's because I was going off of how much the product is worth and not how much my time and energy is worth. At the expo, I showed the one minute clip to a variety of people. I decided to experiment with this concept.

I thought, *Why don't I just test the water and say the product is worth $500, this time?*

I factored in my time and energy as well as all the time it has taken me to teach myself everything I know about video editing. Which, by the way, people don't want to do. Everything I learned about marketing and filmmaking was factored into the cost as well. I also factored in paying my bills and a little bit of a "Fuck You" attitude. I hate getting taken advantage of.

Someone walked by and saw the video and asked me how much it would cost him to have me shoot one for his shop. This was my moment.

I said, "You'd be looking at $500, minimum."

He said, "Are you serious? Why so cheap?"

I was fucking blown away. Even after I increased my own value in my mind, stood my ground, *and* give him a firm base price, he thought it was worth more? A complete stranger, mind you. How do you think that made me feel? It made me feel incredible.

Pulling this right out of my ass, I replied, "I like to make sure I don't put you out of business while I deliver the highest quality product at a price that we both benefit from."

What the fuck was that?

That's what happens. When you know your product inside and out you can bullshit really well. Not as in "lying" really well, but being able to talk and make someone feel like they're amazing or they're getting a great deal based on your expertise.

He said, "I would have thought that was at least $2,000," with a face full of pleasant surprise, "It's *so* cinematic!"

I was like, *Oh My God! Oh My God!*

This made my day. Was my one-minute video clip worth $2,000? Apparently.

That's awesome!

Here's the thing, a total stranger just saw my work and affirmed my value. It was great but what sucked, was the fact that I didn't think *I* was worth that much until *he* said something.

Now, just due to how often these little videos are needed and how fast they are to produce I would never charge that and to be honest, who knows if he would have even paid that. The great part about this, is if I am charging $500, and they think it's worth $2,000, that looks like a 75% discount. Who wouldn't want that for video services?

He just woke me up a little bit. Guess what? I just had a meeting today and we settled on the same sort of social media video for $500. I went into the meeting knowing that my perceived value was really high, and I was able to sell my service for the rate I truly believe it's worth for both parties involved. Will I raise my prices soon? Sure! Just to see what happens.

Another example of this happened at the same expo. I had a business card with an image of a model that I shot for a salon. For this shoot, I charged $800. At the time that was the most money had I made for a photo shoot. The amount of work I ended up having to put into this shoot made me want to rethink my prices. The shoot included eight retouched images and the day of shooting.

Before I gave the client the price, I thought, *Okay, they only want one photo of each model. I can get at least one solid shot in thirty minutes per model.*

It ended up being an hour drive to the location, an hour back, and the shoot day was eight hours long in addition to the drive. On top of that, I estimated the retouching time would take an hour or less to edit each beauty shot. The end result was well over double the estimated time. Needless to say, I learned my lesson. It went from being the most lucrative photo shoot I had ever had, to below my average rate. Since I never wanted this to happen again, I wanted to make sure that I priced it differently if anyone ever asked for a similar shoot.

At the expo, I was showing off the image because I spent so much time on it and it's gorgeous.

Someone walks up and says, "I need that EXACT image but for a dude for my barbershop. I want some editorial images for the shop."

Again, I winged this one, "To get a shot like that, you're looking at $800." I gave no wiggle room.

He said, "Here's my card. I'm serious. I need you, Dude."

He contacted me, not a week after the expo, and we set up a call. He wanted six photos. That's two less than the previous shoot and the best part was that they were of men. Men are a lot easier to photoshop because they wear less makeup and half the image was going to have a beard in it. Therefore, less editing. I didn't have to go in and take all the crap off their chin or jawline.

I told him, "This will cost $1,500!"

I stood my ground and charged a rate that I felt would make me very happy with myself without feeling like I am just in it for the money.

Sounding pleased with the rate, "Okay, let me get back to you in a couple of days and see if we can't set it up."

Sometimes people say that but never respond. He responded to me and I penciled in the date. The shoot ended up being easier than I thought and editing was even easier than the shoot.

Tell me this, how is it possible to be doing less work and getting paid more? It sounded impossible to me as well, until recently. I just started raising my prices and eliminating clients that couldn't pay what I know I'm worth. This is not me trying to fuck over a business or throw out numbers for no reason. I genuinely believe that I'm worth this much based off of all the skills I have acquired over time. It's a mindset. Confidence. You will pay me what I want if I work with you and you will get what you want because of it.

Here is the thing, come to think of it, the clients that have complained the most about my product or services were people that think they could do it themselves or think they are creative enough to give feedback that just doesn't make sense. Those clients were also clients that I gave massive discounts too. They're the ones that wanted more value even after I gave them a ridiculously low price. You'd think it would be the other way around but the clients that have no money, want to bitch and try to get more out of you without paying more. The clients with money, the ones that don't have a hard time paying, value their time like you value your time so they trust that you are giving them the best quality product or service every time. It's just expected. Guess what happens? They don't complain. They may ask for a small revision or an add-on but they also know they are paying extra when they add on. They are fully aware of how this whole thing works. On occasion, you find one that just wants you to keep working but usually those are the ones I charge per hour and it's an hourly rate I don't mind charging. For now. That is going to change. It's strange, but these are life lessons I have had to learn over time as an entrepreneur. Moral of this rant: KNOW YOUR VALUE!!!!

END OF VALUABLE RANT

Back to the original story of this chapter, after working for Chris for a few days, there was just enough work back at AADA for me to work a couple of weeks straight. Since it was still slow during the summer, Joe gave me stupid little tedious tasks partially filling my days. There is nothing more brain numbing than knowing you could be a thousand times more productive but you have to do stupid little tasks that a monkey could do. Have you ever felt that way?

Why am I doing this? This seems beneath my expertise.

Sometimes those little things really need to get done because all of those brain-numbing tasks will equal one large accomplishment. That being said, I would rather just work on a big ass project and have a deadline to hit. Cleaning and organizing is good for someone that wants to make some money and doesn't have the skill set to build an empire. I wanted an empire. I still do. Especially after seeing Chris, not too many years older than myself, own his own business.

I know, you're thinking, *"Isaac, an empire? An empire of what?"*

I didn't quite know at the time but I felt like I could be doing major things in major ways after making major moves. Thus, resulting in some kind of self-made man. It's not cockiness when you're fully aware that you are overqualified for the position you're in. It's the worst feeling. It only took me four or five times to recognize that feeling that kept eating at me. I couldn't put it into words. At the time, I just thought I was a rebellious little shit not wanting to listen to my bosses.

On occasion, I would have a change in location or a change in a project and it would release me from boredom. The majority of the time at work, I would be thinking and dreaming about producing music or writing lyrics down. I would also just daydream about being in the movies or on a billboard. Sometimes I got a little carried away and it felt so real. I can't explain it. Not that I felt better than everyone around me. I just felt as if I was put on this earth to do bigger and better things than everyone around me. If you have the entrepreneurial bug, you know what I mean.

Everyone else says, "This is the way it is. It pays well. There are decent benefits. I have two weeks vacation. What else can you ask for? Living the American Dream."

Since that's what I had heard from the people that I surrounded myself with, I thought, that was the way it was and I had no choice. See, I was torn. I felt like I had no choice but at the same time, I felt like I was in full control of every boss I ever had. It was a strange feeling. I felt like I could run the show if they were gone or I could even put them out of business if I wanted to. Working underneath someone and taking orders just because they write your check and help pay your bills doesn't mean you can't speak your mind and be honest with yourself. If you have this burning desire to be better and accomplish big things, I say go after it. What have you got to lose? You have to understand that there are a million jobs just like the one you're in, right now. If you are in a salary job, you can find another salary job. If you like taking orders from someone that could possibly be younger than you and less skilled, you can always find that again too. There will forever be companies hiring and letting people go. It's a cycle. If you break out of that mold for a little while, I can almost guarantee you will never want to go back to that life.

At the time I didn't know what these feelings were or how to cope with them. I just felt like I was breaking "The Rules" and I was a bad kid because it's frowned upon to think for yourself. See, when you want to learn, companies will teach you. There is an unspoken expectation that you will remain at that company for the remainder of your life because your employer is teaching you the ins and outs of that business. When you start to question authority and make decisions for yourself, you are a liability to the company that has just spent a few thousand dollars compensating you for your time. You are a liability because if you leave with trade secrets, you could help or become their competitor, and put them out of business. That is what they are afraid of. They're afraid of not being able to make money and wasting money on new recruits that could end up leaving and starting their own businesses.

I liked to challenge these "Rules" and ask as many questions about the company as I could by walking around the shops and speaking to my coworkers. I would find out a lot about the business because someone at the top had to vent to someone in the company at some point. There is always some kind of drama in the workplace and you can find it pretty quick because people like to blame others. When it comes to blaming "The Man," it's even easier to acquire information. I was young and I wanted to learn, so these older guys would teach me anything I wanted to learn. I had some guys teaching me about taxes, creating LLCs, setting up bank accounts, how to sell, how to market, how to brand and so much more. It's crazy how much you can learn by asking questions and showing you're interested.

I have never been one to just accept "No!" for an answer. I want to know what gives that muthafuckah that right to tell me, "No!" Is it because it's his or her signature on my pay stub? So fucking what? Is that it? A little doodle of penmanship and all of a sudden you get to give me orders? I don't think so. Why can't I do your job? What do you "know" that I don't in order for me to do what you are doing *AND* do a better job at it? What is it?

These are the kind of things that have been going through my head since I was in high school. Can you relate? If you can, you belong at the top of the food chain with me. If you have a passion for continuously learning or you have a passion to seek out the truth and understand why things are supposed to happen a certain way, you should start your own business. Not to jump too far ahead but that's what I ended up doing on accident. There are plenty of other jobs to discuss and what I learned in each place but I want to start talking about how I started my first business. I feel like it's a good starting point. This is where the real value begins.

11

BECOMING MY OWN BOSS

I t didn't take rocket science to figure out that my actor friends from school, all needed headshots. We were told that we needed headshots to submit to agents, casting directors, directors, and anyone else we wanted to audition for. A headshot is literally just a fancy name for an 8x10 portrait. There are a ton of "rules" that are supposed to be followed in the entertainment industry and I knew this one was something these actors, including myself, would need consistently.

Acquiring knowledge has been fun for me as far back as I can remember. When I was modeling, I would chit chat with the photographers and ask a whole bunch of questions.

They looked at me like, "Stupid model. He's just a pretty face. I suppose I could entertain his questions. He's not a photographer stealing my 'trade secrets'. What's the worst that could happen?"

This was before Youtube was a place you could learn anything you wanted to learn. I would ask them questions about the camera, lenses, lighting setups, clouds, etc. It wasn't because I wanted to be a photographer at the time, it was simply because I love to learn. Since I had been asking these questions for years and years, I picked up on a few different things. Especially when it came to poses and little techniques to familiarize the model with the camera and their environment. Whether it was laughter, joking, or house music in the background, there were a bunch of little things done to me that I knew I liked and disliked about a photoshoot.

I'm very comfortable in front of the camera but not everyone can say the same thing and I know that. I also had communication skills. All I needed now, was to buy a camera and learn how to use it.

It takes photos, right? It can't be that hard.

I knew a couple of goofballs back in Massachusetts that shot and they weren't even close to the brightest bulbs. I knew I was going to be able to do a better job than they could. All I had to do was learn.

Right around this time, I was still working at AADA and I had befriended a kid named Matthew Stannah. He is an amazing actor. (We almost became roommates at one point. That's another story for another time. We both thought each other played for the other team because we both looked pretty and got on well with the ladies. Come to find out, neither of us were gay and we became really great friends. Not that if either of us were gay, we wouldn't have been good Friends. We were just used to other men hitting on us and we wanted to avoid that if we could. I'll still hit on Matt just to fuck with him.) Anyways, we got to talking and we both realized that he needed headshots. I said, "I'll take them for you."

He was a little worried about my expertise and skill set, but he still agreed. I worked my ass off for a few weeks and saved up a couple of hundred dollars. One day, on a Friday, my boss never came in and I told Matt, "I'll be back in a bit."

He didn't care because our boss was out and Matt got to play "Boss" that day.

"See ya soon," he said.

I ran as fast as I could down 32nd street and headed straight to B&H which is my favorite store on this planet. It's a Toys 'R Us for filmmakers, photographers, and musicians. If you ever get the chance to visit, do it. They have a conveyor belt that runs up along the ceiling, from all the customer service desks and it leads straight to the front of the store. You don't have to carry anything around while purchasing big pieces of equipment. It waits for you up front and you can just grab it as you leave. I had never seen anything like it. Someone told me to check it out if I was buying a camera, so I did. I walked in and asked for some help finding the digital camera section.

I told the guy, "I need a camera that shoots both photo and video. I want to start a production company."

He asked what my budget was, and I said "$600."

He must have thought I was out of my mind and sent me upstairs to talk to one of the guys up there. I said the same thing to the guys upstairs and they introduced me to the Sony SLT-a57. I had no idea what it was but it was in my price range and he said it shot both video and photos.

I thought, *Perfect, I can shoot Matt's headshots now and maybe shoot a sketch or something.*

I bought the camera and it came with a kit lens that was a 3.5-5.6, 18-55mm. It had auto-focus and it zoomed. I thought that was cool.

The sales rep up-sold me on some UV filters that I hated because it ended up leaving a bright green flare on my images and it would be a reflection of whatever was in front of the lens. It was really weird. I found out why, and how that happened later on. This is why you need to know what you want and don't let other people persuade you.

I remember sprinting back to school because I was so happy and I wanted to show Matt. As if he knew what the fuck it was or how good or bad it was going to be. At that moment, I didn't care. The sky was the limit for what I was about to do with this camera.

I even told him, "Dude, we can shoot movies now!"

He loved that idea because he *was* and still *is* an amazing writer. He's also quite the dreamer. That's another thing we have in common. I took the camera home and begged my blue-eyed, girlfriend, to be my first test dummy for the "portrait" setting. I didn't even know what "manual" was at that point. I knew that the little "M" on the dial was the one that seemed to confuse me most. My girlfriend had such gorgeous blue eyes every picture I took made me look like a professional, instantly. I soon found out that I had no idea what I was doing when I started reaching out to other friends and asking them to let me take their picture.

I shot brown eyes, red hair, balding, beards, clean shaven, beautiful people, unattractive people, and even puppies. After all that, I still had no idea what I was doing. The issue was that I wasn't using "Manual Mode." For someone that likes to be in full control of everything I touch, equating to large amounts of freedom in my mind, I was beyond frustrated and pretty upset when I couldn't get the exact picture I wanted. I wanted more blur. That was probably my most consistent request.

"Father, I want more Blur! Make it blurrier, Father!" (Reread that in a British accent while you stick your nose straight up to the sky. It will help get my point across.)

In my mind, all my favorite movies had city lights or string lights behind the actor's head that were all blurred out. At the time, *"blur"* was the only word I knew. Thanks to Google, I took it upon myself to learn more about this "vision of blur" that I wanted so badly. Luckily, there were a couple of amazing photographers or should I say, "Youtube Teachers," that keyworded the words *"Blur"* and *"Bokeh"* in the same video. I swear, if it wasn't for Google and Youtube, I wouldn't be where I am today. Those two sites, in particular, changed my entire outlook on life. They tested my boundaries of knowledge and challenged my curiosity to learn.

It's a funny thing, the interweb. You click one little blue, underlined, and highlighted word or phrase and hours later you find yourself on web pages that probably should have been reported to the FBI long before you landed on it. In this case, the word blur was not so provocative and I found exactly what I was looking for, shortly after searching for it. The look that I was going for was called "Shallow Depth of Field". Who knew? If you look at any of my photography or watch any of my cinematography work, you'll find my style rather quickly.

Again, because I like being in control of everything, I like directing my viewer's attention. Whether they want to look there or not, I don't give them a choice. They actually make special effects that you can buy, or presets you can add to your image or footage, to achieve something similar, if you somehow forgot your desired style on the day of shooting.

When you have a shallow depth of field, the lens focuses on whatever you adjust the focus to, blurring out everything else around it. Sometimes, this is not good. This is a lesson I learned rather quickly. What's the first thing you do when you get a new toy? What's the first thing you do when you get a new phone or computer? You dive right in until you are familiar with your new surroundings. Sometimes you dive in so fast that you get bored even quicker after figuring it out so quickly. That's almost what happened to me.

I never got bored though. However, I did dive right in and at every stage of learning, I felt like I fully understood the basics and could call myself a professional. This happened every time I learned something new. I wasn't even comparing videos that I watched to create my own style. I was literally copying other people's styles and saying they were my own. I say, "copying," but if you were to compare the two, my work looked nothing like it because I was fucking horrible, truth be told. Here's why: I learned that one little dial would give me my desired outcome and I would only play with that dial. I had no idea that you had to adjust three dials every single time you want to take a series of pictures to properly expose the image. This left me with unusable images. Even after running through photoshop, which I used the same way, sliding sliders all the way and destroying my product faster than my shutter closing.

"Shutter," another word I had no clue about. We'll discuss the dials in detail another time. I just knew that I liked the *"Bokeh Look."* The dial that controlled that look was called the "Aperture" or "F-Stop."

I love when I come across four hundred words that all mean the same exact thing. It's amazing. It's super easy to learn that way.

If I could use a red-faced emoji right now, I would.

Why can't we just use one term? I don't get it.

When I moved over to cinema lenses, their specs said "T" and no longer said "F"? Another learning curve. It literally means that same exact shit when you dumb it down. So now I have, *"Blur"* and *"Bokeh"* meaning the same thing, and I have "Aperture" and "F-Stop" that I need to adjust to get the "blurry bokeh effect."

Does that mean I adjust two dials? Wait! I am so confused!

Youtube, once again saved me from going insane. It was just one dial. You'd think that was easy right? One dial, no big deal. I was shooting all my friends in the middle of the day when the sun is at its brightest. I would crank this little dial all the way down to F3.5 and not adjust any other setting. I would essentially be taking a completely white photo. You couldn't even see my friends in the image. Especially my British friends.

What was even more confusing was that the lens that came with the camera, the kit lens, was a zoom lens. It only came with one lens. I was taking portraits with an 18-55mm lens. The blurriest my lens could get was at F3.5 and that was only when it was zoomed out all the way to 18mm. This meant that the only way to capture what I thought I wanted was to get extremely close to their face. Even though we were friends and all, this still made both of us really uncomfortable. Even my own girlfriend was freaked out. Since this was a new issue that needed resolving, I decided to zoom in and max out my zoom. That way I was able to stand further away. There were no in-betweens when I was learning. It was always one extreme or the other. Sometimes I still take that same approach. I find that I fail quicker and by doing so, I learn my lesson much faster. When I zoomed in to try and correct this problem and make my future clients happy, I watched my subject get darker as more and more of the background came into focus. This infuriated me.

What the fuck was I doing wrong? I thought, *This doesn't make any sense.*

After countless hours of research and adjusting my camera settings to manual, and back and forth to automatic, I found the issue. I ended up Googling the exact lens and numbers on my lens to find images I could compare to. It took me ages to figure out that my lens *automatically* adjusted the aperture to F5.6 when I zoomed in. Thus allowing more to be in focus and making the image darker. It was only when I Googled, 18-55mm 3.5-5.6, that I came across something that explained it to me. This made me even more pissed off because I was doing things right in my mind, but even while I was shooting manual, there were still automatic settings?

WHY?

Then, my life changed. I wanted to throw away the lens because it would never give me the desired look I was going for. According to the reference images for each setting of the lens, I was using the wrong lens. Being so fed up, I Googled, "Best lens for Portraits. Best lens for headshots. Best lens for depth of field." Anything that would bring me closer to what I wanted. I came across a variety of options, as you would imagine. Prices ranging from $300 to $5,000. I started looking at the lenses that were way past my budget, naturally.

Damn, $300? Why so expensive?

Seriously, at the time $300 was an astronomical amount of money to save up. As I said before, it was at least a couple of weeks worth of work and a couple more weeks worth of saving. The funny thing was, I went off of the price and not the specs at first. When I went off of specs, I came across a lens that was a 50mm, F1.8. I was assuming it didn't zoom. I was also assuming it wouldn't get darker, for no fucking reason, as well. I'm sorry, it's not for no reason, the reason is I didn't have enough money to buy a zoom lens that remained at a constant "Aperture" throughout the entirety of the zoom process. They definitely make them but I was too broke to afford what I was looking for. I didn't find that out until later on. Right around the time, I realized eBay was an amazing option for buying used lenses and camera gear.

Anyways, I found a lens that seemed to be what I was looking for. Everyone said that 50mm was a nice length because it was very close to what your eye naturally sees as far as distance goes. It had less warp; the whole thing. I also knew that the lower the F-Stop, the more *"Blur"* or *"Bokeh,"* I would end up with.

I thought, *The lower, the better, for me.*

The lowest I saw was actually F1.1 or something ridiculous but it was more of a microscope than anything else. At a certain point, it is definitely possible to have pretty close to...not a damn thing in focus. Again, from Google Images, I saw what I was looking for and it was the 50mm, F1.8.

I thought, *Great. Sounds good. When can I get this?*

It was back to pinching pennies all over again.

When I had enough money, I waited for my boss to leave early again. I pulled another half day and ran over to B&H on

34th street, as fast I could. (GO THERE!! It's amazing!! Have I said that already?) I ran upstairs and this time I knew where I was going because I was a "professional" now. I approached the same Sony Kiosk that had sold me last time.

The sales rep said, "You're in the wrong area. Head over there. You see that line? You'll get called when a space at the counter opens up."

Amateur hour all over again.

"Thank you, sir."

I waited in line for my turn to ask a whole bunch of questions. Here was another "professional" move: I left my camera at home.

What better place to test the lens before purchasing? Good Job, Isaac!

A neon sign, a few counter spaces down, started blinking. It was my turn. I knew what I wanted anyway so it wasn't the end of the world, I just couldn't test the lens.

To be honest I didn't know that was an option until the sales rep asked me if I brought my camera. It was a subtle way of him saying, "You're asking too many questions, Kid. It's better to see for yourself but your dumbass left it at home."

I told him which one I wanted because I memorized it, obviously. This was back before my phone did all the memorizing for me.

He searched through their inventory and said, "Sorry, we're out of stock."

No, he didn't say that. That would have been awful.

"Is there anything else I can get you? How about a UV Filter?" That's what he actually said.

Not learning my lesson from last time, "Sounds good," and he up-sold me on the UV Filter once again.

Damn, they're so good at their job.

The employees, in the basement, sifted through the stock and sent up a little orange box and a small plastic case with a UV Filter.

Oh, look. A UV Filter.

I remember looking at it as my sales rep gently placed it in another box on the magical ceiling system, letting the conveyor belt do the rest of the hard labor. I just watched my hard earned money disappear and I didn't even stick up for myself.

What a weak, weak, man.

It's wasn't too costly but that extra little bit of money would have been better spent on food to feed my broke ass. I walked out of the store feeling like such a professional. I did my research and got what I wanted. Finally, something I was going to be able to control. When I got back to AADA, instead of working, I stared at the little orange box and dreamt about my camera thirty blocks uptown.

Later that evening, I asked my girlfriend to be my test dummy again. She was game. Her eyes never looked so good. After all the research and forcing myself to learn manual settings, I was able to control everything about the image. I was stoked. I left that lens wide open at F1.8 for months while I was shooting her and my friends, once again.

It was time, I could start asking my friends if they wanted headshots. It started off just testing lighting, settings, and small things. Now it was time to actually try shooting for a reason. I wanted to help my friends by giving them "professional" headshots. There was one problem: Nobody wanted them done, even for free, because I was so bad. They remembered that the last images were straight garbage and they didn't want to go through that again. Fair enough, I couldn't blame them.

Finally, I had a few friends agree to let me try again. That was all I needed. Since they were friends, we would be laughing the whole time and the shots looked great...during playback. When I offloaded the images and started organizing them on my hard drive, I noticed that my subjects were out of focus. Not by much but as I said before, it is possible to have most of the image out of focus when you are shooting with such a low F-Stop. I really only noticed it after I went through the images, deleted the goofy, unusable ones, and sent them to my "clients." The client would be super happy and pick their favorites. I'd proceed to bring them into photoshop to give them a quick touch up. Which ended up never being as quick as I was hoping.

As I was about to begin manipulating their facial features, for the better, I noticed that the eyeballs were totally out of focus. As in, unusable if printed larger than wallet size. Not only did this mean that I had to tell my client that we couldn't use their favorite picks, but I had to go through all the images again. I had to eliminate the blurry eyed images so it would never happen again.

That's the worst, telling your friend or client, "We can't use the image you love so very much, because I don't know how to do my job. Sorry."

Okay, so I figured out that I need to shoot a little higher than F1.8 to get more than just eyelashes in focus. Cool, I got this.

Next on the problematic list was explaining why they don't get all the images that were taken on the day of the shoot.

"What's a proof," they'd ask, or, "I want to post these. Do you mind?"

Of course, I mind. The image that comes straight out of the camera is not my final product. Why would I want you showing the world fifty percent of what I can do?

I politely responded, "Please, do not post the images that I've sent you to choose from. They are not the final edits."

"That's okay. I don't mind," they'd say, "I just love them so much."

NO! Goddamnit! What is wrong with you? That was the exact thought that crossed my mind, every time. I never said it, obviously.

It was time to create a real proof that they wouldn't want to post as soon as they saw it because it would *look* unfinished. That was the new plan. Originally, I would get rid of thirty to forty photos of them blinking or moving their hair out of the way. Pictures they would never be able to use, ever.

However, because I said to them at the end of the shoot, "Wow, we shot over four hundred photos today," they would be very confused when they received anything less than that. So, I decided to come up with a plan. The plan was to stop telling them how many images we shot on the day of shooting. Then, I would get rid of all the junk photos. Sometimes I'd save the candid ones that looked really cool. After that, I would place a see-through watermark on every single photo that remained, and at the same time, I would resize the images and make them so small that they would never be able to print it or post it online because it would look like shit. This process worked well for a little while and then people started complaining about not being able to see the entire image.

They started asking me, "Why does it look so blurry when I zoom in?"

Once again, I messed up. There is no middle ground for me, so what ended up happening was I'd place four or five watermarks saying, "© Isaac Danna Photography-PROOF" all over the proofs. This really did make it impossible to post or print but it also made it really hard to get a feel for the image. *I couldn't even tell if I liked it or not and that's what all the clients thought as well. They were having issues with it.*

Happy clients meant more business in the future. The only thing I wanted to do was keep this entire ordeal as simple as possible. There had to be a middle ground where we would both be happy. I would make sure they saw an unfinished product *and* they would be able to pick which unfinished product they would like me to complete. Sounds simple right?

Why was this so hard?

I took off four watermarks and left one right across the middle of the image, at an angle. You couldn't Photoshop it out if you tried. I lighten it up enough to see every part of the image while still establishing the fact the product was not final at this point. It was only there for viewing and selection. This was it! This worked. I was also able to find a speech for the end of our shoots. I found a process that made both of us happy. It was a no brainer.

To be honest, this is still my process. I still get requests to post the proofs to social media but my reply has changed, "Yeah, no problem. I don't mind you posting it but just make sure to state that it's a proof, unedited, or raw image."

That works wonders. More happy customers. I told you that it's still what I do to this day and that's awesome. What I haven't told you yet: there was a moment where I actually had to change the process a little more on my end so I could keep clients even happier. I am a firm believer in failure. If you aren't failing, you aren't working hard enough and you aren't experimenting enough. When I first started shooting, and editing, I had to figure it all out on my own. I had no idea what a mentor was and I probably wouldn't have listened anyway. This was a very hard lesson to learn.

One of the first paying customers I had, was a friend from acting school. She needed new headshots and she came to me. I was cheap, but you get what you pay for. I didn't know my worth and I felt that my product wasn't quite worth more than $150. Mind you, this is New York City. Headshot sessions would cost upwards of $1,200 depending on where you would go to get them done. We had a great day of shooting. We were laughing, smiling, joking around and capturing all of it. It was perfect. I got home and went through my process. This time in particular, I sent her the proofs really quickly because she was paying and I didn't have any other gigs preventing me from completing the session.

I figured, *Why not just send them over right after the shoot? She can pick within a few hours and my turnaround time will be really fast.*

In theory, I was trying to make sure that my $150 shoot didn't take up more of my time than I wanted it to. If I could make $150 for 8 hours of work, that was worth it for me when i first started. That's disgusting money, now. I know my worth, now.

Later on that evening I received an email from my client with her favorite choices and I got straight to work. As I searched through the folders to find the original files from the shoot, the ones without the watermarks, the high-resolution ones for editing and printing, I couldn't find them. I searched for about an hour in the same three folders. I grabbed my memory card out of my camera and slid it in and out of my Mac's SD slot, over and over, until I nearly broke my card. The card was empty. Nothing was showing up.

What happened was, I formatted it right after transferring the images from the shoot to my computer. I had a folder on my computer with the client's name. Then, inside that folder were two more folders, one labeled "Proofs," and the other labeled "JPEGS." It wasn't making sense, I looked at the "JPEG" folder over and over trying to figure out why all the "original images" had watermarks on them. I was so confused. The "Proofs" folder was empty. Completely empty. I don't know if you're following along here but I would usually grab the images from the card, drop all four hundred of them in a folder called "JPEGS" and then go into Photoshop, add the watermark, resize them, and then resave them as new, smaller files. Then, I'd lower the quality and label that folder, "Proofs." In this case, when I went to save all the proofs, I accidentally wrote over the original images in the process. I forgot to pick the proper folder so that wouldn't happen. It was already bad enough that I was editing JPEGs and not RAW images or TIFF images. I didn't know that at the time. I'll explain the difference later.

After searching for hours and finding out that I couldn't even start over if I wanted to because I totally erased my memory card, I just wanted to cry. I didn't want to tell my client that the entire day was a waste of her time and money. I felt horrible. I had to come up with my apology, my game plan on how I intended to fix this problem, and what my next move was. After a few more hours of thinking out loud and yelling at myself, I came up with a solution. I would start with telling her the bad news, right away, just to get it out of the way. Then, I would solve the issue before she even has a chance to think about other solutions or ask for her money back.

I called her up and apologized, "I am so sorry. This never happened before and I feel awful. I want to make it up to you and shoot again for free. This will not happen again, I swear, and I will make sure I give you an extra edit."

I explained what happened and she appreciated my honesty and willingness to correct my mistake. She agreed to the new terms, not entirely sure that this wouldn't happen again, but trusting me to come through. I did. I came through. We rescheduled the next shoot and I made sure to take my time to process the images properly.

I will say that she never hired me again and I don't blame her, but she loved the images from the second shoot more than the first shoot anyways. It ended up working out in the end. In addition to capturing better images in round two, I learned a massive lesson on how to organize photos and projects and how to never, ever, press "format" until the project is completed, or unless I have made several copies and practically locked my originals in a digital safe somewhere.

It was right around this time that I was bragging about my newly found photographer skill set and I was posting all of my work to Facebook.

One day, a photographer friend of mine, who actually went to college to be a photographer, sent me a private message saying, "So, you're a photographer now?"

I didn't know how to take it. *Was she jealous? Was she pissed that I was making money and she wasn't? Was she a little ticked off about wasting money on college courses just to have a competitor entirely self-taught?*

To this day, I still don't know. In fact, most of the photographers that used to shoot me when I was modeling, don't even talk to me now. Ever since I started publishing my work, they saw it as competition or they would try to give me some advice on how to shoot but in a "Hey, fuckhead, you're not a photographer," kind of way.

With that being said, the photographer that I referenced earlier, who paid for college to learn what she could have learned online, messaged me with another one-liner that I found degrading.

"Try lowering the opacity!"

I didn't even know what opacity was, so I had to Google it. I was used to coming across words that I was unfamiliar with so I didn't really mind. After hours of research, I assumed she meant, "Lower the opacity of my retouched layers and effects."

I was correct. In this case, she was actually trying to help me but because she didn't fully explain herself and just jabbed my throat, I had to figure it out. To be perfectly honest, that probably helped me more. In the end, I really had to research what she meant by it. This was a turning point in my photography career. Again, there is no in between for me.

As I said before, the sliders in Photoshop were either all the way at one hundred percent or nothing at all. This was a huge mistake on my end because you could clearly tell, even after creating what I thought to be a transparent editing process, the images were "Photoshopped." That's absolutely the worst kind of Photoshopping, when you think to yourself, *Damn, that person is Photoshopped.*

That is the very reason I tried to learn how to edit in a transparent way. I didn't want you to see my edits. I took this to heart because, once again, I felt like a failure and I attempted to make it right. It was time for me to play with the middle of the sliders and lower the opacity. I started off around ninety percent instead of a hundred. It still looked Photoshopped. I kept dropping it until I couldn't notice it as much. It took ages for me to figure out the happy medium where I could manage the layers in such a way that it seemed very natural. To this day, I still have a hard time doing it and I sit there sliding those sliders till the cows come home. It's never, ever one hundred percent perfect and it drives me nuts. Retouching is an art form and it's subjective. I have had clients actually ask me to make them skinnier. If I showed you the before and after, *"HOLY SHIT!"*

I would bet the farm on you saying, "Holy shit, Dude. Chill out on the editing. That's not right. She looks a Barbie."

The old saying, "The Customer Is Always Right," stood true in this case. I even showed my client the before and after and she was ecstatic. It's odd how every person is different. It took me a while to learn that. Some customers want their moles removed, some want their nose adjusted--it's insane--some want their tits bigger, (I don't mind doing that, though. Those are the fun ones.) and some want to post the fucking proofs and call it a day. It's mind-blowing. I've learned to just accept what they want and throw my own little flare on it so it still bears some resemblance of my own work. Know what I mean?

.   .   .

So, after all this talk about quitting my job on multiple occasions, chasing my dream, begging friends, and learning lessons, I forgot to tell you that Matthew Stannah and I have yet to have a headshots session together. That was the whole point of buying this camera in the first place. Well, one of them anyways. I have used the camera with him and he has taken my headshot with it, oddly enough, but I haven't taken his. He was the first one I offered them to and he knew I sucked so he never took me up on the offer. Way to go, Matt! However, about a year ago, after my skill level increased significantly, he reached out and asked me to set up a package deal with him and his wife. Funny how he didn't want headshots until he knew I wouldn't shoot them for free anymore. Even after we set that shoot up, I ended up only shooting his wife and the rescheduling of his session never happened. It's hilarious to me. Still, to this day, I find it humorous.

12

THE PRICING CHALLENGE

W hen I created my very first business, taking an actor's headshots, I had a *very* big problem when it came to pricing. I had no idea where to begin. Legit, I just created magical numbers out of thin air. Giving no regard to the cost of equipment, software, travel expenses, or (most importantly) my time. I mentioned earlier about knowing your self-worth and the worth of your product or service; it's by far one of the most important lessons I have learned. You'd think people would at least give you a chance and take advantage of free products and services but for some reason, they didn't.

In the modeling world, models and photographers would trade services and shoot on a TFP basis, TFP meaning "Trade For Print." As the digital age started evolving, nobody needed prints and it became TF. "Trade For…" whatever was agreed upon; digital images, flash drives, or CDs of all the images, you name it. This is how models and photographers both created their portfolios when they first started out. Photographers would be able to test lighting and new techniques and models would have new photos to show agents and casting directors. It's a no brainer when you're both helping each other out.

With acting, it was a little different. People only wanted the best headshot, and because actors aren't exactly models, a lot of actors that I was working with were not comfortable in front of the camera. They assumed that the photographer would make that fear disappear if they paid top dollar. So, in their eyes, a photographer just starting out would not have enough experience dealing with shy actors and it would be a waste of their time altogether. It's kind of understandable. Models are used to posing for the camera and ending up with stunning images every time. Even an amateur model is in front of a camera a lot more than an amateur actor, and because not all actors are as attractive as models they are worried about what they'll look like on screen. They could have the most talent in the room or on the set, but they're just worried about how they look and they expect the photographer to make them comfortable enough to look sexy. This made it very difficult to approach actors and ask them if they wanted free headshots. They assumed I didn't know what I was doing. I had plenty of images of family and friends that I would showcase to prove that I did know I could at least take their headshot. Still, nobody wanted them. Maybe one or two people but that was only because they were super desperate.

As soon as I started charging $50 for a shoot, however, I had doubled the amount of people interested. It didn't make sense in my brain but I decided to try again and come up with a "deal" for $100. They bit. Then I raised it to $150. The client after that, $250. I just kept raising it. When I hit $300, it was a "yes," every time. When I hit $350 it was almost 200% more likely than $300, if that's even possible.

During this period of time my girlfriend, who had been my girlfriend and not been my girlfriend quite often, was recommending me to her friends and what not. Even when we weren't together. One kid hit me up and asked how much. I knew that he had been trying to talk to my girlfriend when we were "on a break."

I said, "Hey, Bro, thanks for reaching out. Headshot sessions are $450..."

I had to jack the price up for this little fucker because he was chattin' up my girl. He knew me too, so that's what really set me off.

"Awesome, man. When are you free?" He said.

HOLY SHIT! I thought to myself, *Did he just agree to this ridiculous price?*

He did. That's when I found out that my quality was worth at least $450 to my customer. The shoot wasn't awkward because I don't like making things awkward and I wanted to keep it professional. The best part about this shoot was that I was getting paid the most I had made for my photography and by the end of the shoot, I got one of my favorite photos at the time. This was back in 2013, and the whole shoot felt like a stepping stone for me.

By now, I was confident enough to charge $350-$450 every time and come up with packages that would include a different number of edits depending on what the potential client wanted. I don't believe it's the kind of industry where you can create cookie cutter prices and just dish them out. The reason for that is each client has their own needs. I'd give them a *ballpark* figure right off the *bat*. (Haven't had one of those Dad Jokes in a while, huh?)

When they adjusted the quantity of retouches they wanted or the number of looks, I would also adjust the price accordingly. Prices became more personal and not so, "This is what I charge for everyone."

It may not seem fair but in the end, some people had lower budgets and I would design a package that included as much as I could for the price they wanted to pay. It worked out for both of us.

That's how my pricing still works today. We haven't spoken much about filmmaking yet, but every single project is different depending on the complexity. In order to give the most accurate price you really need to try and figure out exactly what it's going to take to produce the project. Not to beat a dead horse here, but after a while I learned that if one client would live an hour away, the next client would live 20 minutes away, one client would like to shoot for 30 minutes, and another type of client enjoyed sucking up every minute, of every hour, of every day. How are you supposed to charge them the same rate? I had to start coming up with systems to put time limits on sessions and even then, people would really push it until the very last second.

I never wrote these questions down and I should have but every time I was speaking to a potential customer, I would ask them a few questions: "Where would you like to shoot? How many retouches do you want? How many outfits do you want to wear? Do you want hair and makeup for the shoot or will you do it yourself? Are you using these images for your website, printing them out, or both? Will you be bringing someone with you?"

Each one of these questions had a purpose. It would help me understand what I was getting myself into. If they were bringing someone with them, I would charge a little bit more. Why? Because it's obnoxious when someone's interrupting constantly, trying to help but becoming more of a burden. If the client wanted five different hairstyles, four changes of clothes and four edits while my previous client wanted one hairstyle, one retouch, and one change of clothes, it becomes very clear which customer I would end up spending the majority of my time on.

Don't get me wrong, this strategy wasn't created overnight. I would just keep track of all the shit that annoyed me about a client, take the blame, and adjust accordingly on the next one. A perfect combination of giving the *client* the exact result they wanted while charging a rate that made *me* happily put in the amount of work needed to make *them* happy is how I designed my packages.

13

REWARDED

Apparently, whatever I was doing was working. Slowly, of course, but it was still working. I couldn't complain. I was working at AADA, Desigual, and now shooting photos for people. It wasn't just headshots anymore, either. I had some people who wanted me to shoot the dress rehearsals for their plays. Matt Stannah, Yudelka Heyer, and I put up a play Matt wrote, in an Off-Off-Broadway theatre, in Times Square. I took photos just to remember how awesome the experience was, and these photos ended up being used in a few online review blogs that circulated the theatrical community. Blogs were becoming the new newspaper. It was where people would find upcoming performances and productions in the local community. This was the biggest thing for me at the time. I was able to show people I was "published" by sending them reference links, and soon other writers and producers started reaching out to me and asking me to capture their rehearsals as well.

Matt was acting in a play outside of our African Inspired

Theatre Company, *Red Soil Productions*. He called me up and said, "Hey buddy, would you do me a favor and shoot some photos for a play I'm in?"

I said, "Possibly. What's the rate and where is it?"

It was paying small money but it wasn't too far away from where I was living in Manhattan at the time. I agreed to shoot the rehearsal and penciled him in. When the date came, the only thing I kept thinking about was getting paid. Nothing else mattered at the time because I was struggling financially. (Like the rest of artist friends) It was a small, black box theatre with not many seats. It was another Off-Off-Broadway theatre in the Lower East Side. I didn't have much room to run around and take photos and it was extremely dark in this theatre as the director wanted the play to be very dramatic. Luckily, I bought that lens with the "epic blur" that I was dreaming about and another added benefit was that the lower the F-Stop, the more light I could let in. This resulted in brighter pictures than a phone could take. I was taking photos in really low light and because it was a performance, no flashes were allowed. Phones at the time couldn't take pictures as good in low light. The only other person shooting photos during the play had a little point and shoot camera that was absolutely terrible.

I really enjoyed the play and it inspired me to take better photos as the shoot progressed. In the end, I was told by the woman paying me, to give my memory card to the guy with the point and shoot camera. I never give all my photos away because I can't control the outcome. I learned my lesson in the past. People posted my images and it wasn't representing the high-quality of my work. In this case, I felt like I was being taken advantage of when she asked me to deliver all of the images before she wrote the check. I was a little bitch in the moment and just did as she said, not sticking up for myself. I had no idea who the other dude was and why he had a camera if they were hiring me as the photographer anyways. It didn't make any sense. She wrote me a check after that and I went on my way after my memory card was offloaded and back in my possession.

About a week later, I stopped at a bar around the corner from AADA, where all my peers would hang out after class. Matt was there and we were having a laugh, drinking away our hard earned money. He was in quite a funky mood. A few drinks in, I was pretty drunk and one drink away from slurring my speech.

Matt said, "Bro, how exciting is this?"

I was like, "What? What are you talking about?"

"The paper!"

"What paper, dude?"

He looked at me and suddenly realized I had no clue what he was on about. "Oh shit! I didn't tell you? Sorry, bro!"

"Matt, what happened?" I thought he got his Visa or something because he's African and Irish and he was applying for a work visa around that same time in the US.

He said, "Your picture made it into the New York Times, Bro! I fucking love you!"

At this point, I still had no idea what he was talking about because I was so drunk. "The Times? What picture, dude?"

"You know, the one from the other night," he said.

Nope!

I still had no idea what he was saying. After begging him to dumb it down for little drunk man, he explained that the guy with the point and shoot camera was in PR. They hired him to take some snapshots in case they couldn't get a photographer in time and he would come up with some review materials and press packets for the media. What happened was, one of my photos ended up being one of the best ones. That just so happened to be the one he submitted to the Times for the Art section.

I said, "Are you serious? Dude, I need a copy. It was in today's?"

"Yeah! It was in today's paper!"

"Did you get me a copy?"

"I didn't have enough money on me, Bro. Sorry!"

As I looked at my watch, I realized it was the next morning. We were out so late and the evening just disappeared. I remember thinking to myself, *Fuck! Fuck! Fuck! Where can I find a copy now? The papers will all be replaced within the hour, if not already.*

"I'll be back," I told Matt, as I sprinted to the nearest deli.

They were out. I ran to the next deli. They were out. I ran in and out of at least five or six places trying to find yesterday's newspaper. I ended up running into CVS around 12:30 am. I looked at the newspaper rack and there they were.

I thought, *Today's paper. Wait! No! That's yesterday's date at the top.*

They didn't just have one copy, they had three copies. One for my mom, one for my grandmother and one for myself. This was perfect. I grabbed them and played defense all the way to the counter as if someone else in the store was trying to get the same three copies because they were filled with solid gold nuggets or something. I never even looked inside. I could have bought the wrong one. That wasn't my first thought, though. My first thought was, *They have them! I'm stealing the entire rack and putting it in my bedroom!*

As I approached the counter, the cashier looked at me funny. Maybe it was the ear to ear grin on my face. I'm not too sure.

She said, "Did you find what you were looking for?"

I said, "You have no idea!"

Then I thought, *Wait! Did I find what I was looking for?*

Now, I had to double check. The line was extending behind me as I gently fingered my way through to the Arts and Entertainment section.

There it is! Nope! That's not my image.

I flipped through the entire section and as I turned the right side of the page over to close the section, there it was. It wasn't the first image but it did take up a huge chunk of real estate on the back page. It was above the fold, which I now know is a very important place to be, after learning advertising and marketing years later.

I told the cashier, "This is my photo!"

She didn't believe me. I had to show her the name on my debit card so she knew it matched the credited photographer's name under the bottom right side of the photograph in the paper. Once I proved my point, she was just as happy as I was about it.

"Woah! Congratulations. That's amazing! Good for you!"

I was almost speechless at this point. Especially after seeing my own photography printed in one of the biggest newspapers in the United States. Can you imagine? It wasn't an obituary sized photo. I mean, it took up half the page. I ran out of CVS after spending the last of my money on these three copies. I was so happy. Even as I write this little bit, I'm recalling the exact emotions I had at that time.

Once I found my way back to the bar, I put the bag down and called my grandmother. None of this would have happened without my grandmother and grandfather's help. I would never, ever, call them so late at night but this was a special occasion for me. They co-signed my student loans so I could chase my dreams in New York City. (Whatever those dreams were. They may have been morphing into something else.) I would have never had this experience if it wasn't for them believing in me. I know this doesn't sound like a huge deal but when I never even thought about having my photography in a newspaper, it blew my mind. I was on cloud nine. Mind you, I was still drunk. That's probably why it took me so long to find the copies if I'm honest.

My grandmother was asleep when I called and I knew that she would be, so I left a message. "Gram, I love you so much! Thank you! Thank you," plus a whole lot of other sappy shit I can't remember because I was too hammered. When I'm drunk I get super emotional and that combined with the feeling of gratitude ended up leaving my grandmother with an extra long voicemail.

Being Gram and all, she called me back about *two* days later. When I finally spoke with her, I said, "Why didn't you call me back sooner?"

"Isaac, you sounded so drunk, I figured you'd need at least *one* day to recover."

That was embarrassing but wicked funny. She knew exactly what I needed and how happy I was.

14

FILM MY MONOLOGUE

D ay in and day out, I was surrounded by actors and future playwrights. Remember how I told you that I bought a camera that could shoot video and photo? The time had come for me to shoot some video with it. Once again, who better to shoot than Matt, right? He just so happened to have an audition, but he wanted to be really lazy and he didn't actually want to attend the audition.

Why would you attend an audition if you could submit a self-tape from the comfort of your own home?

He asked me if I would shoot a monologue he had prepared and asked if I could shoot it in a "cinematic way."

Whatever that meant.

He came over one day and I sat him down in a chair, not too far from a big glass door that allowed for amazingly soft light. He wasn't nervous at all. In fact, I was more nervous than he was. I pressed the little red button on my Sony and began recording.

"Action," I said.

He began his monologue with ease and I followed the flow, trying to keep my camera as steady as possible with my hands. I freehanded the entire piece. If I'm not mistaken, we shot it a few times just to be safe. After we both agreed that he had nailed the part, we offloaded the files and picked the best take. We chose the best clip and I imported it into Premiere Pro. At the time, I had no idea what I was doing. I would just experiment with sliders, as I did in Photoshop, and completely mess up the clip. I got so frustrated with what I was doing, I told him that I would figure something out after he left. I hate learning when someone's watching over my shoulder. He left and I decided that I would learn as much as I could about editing video, as fast as I could. It was back to the drawing board. Google, once again, became my best friend.

"Premiere Pro cinematic editing"
"How to edit like a movie"
"DIY cinematic look"
"Tips and tricks for cinematic look"

Eventually, I found what I was looking for. Sometimes you need to have a little bit of patience to see where your curiosity takes you. After manipulating the sliders in such a way and playing with color wheels, I finally found a "look" that stood apart from your regular "HD video quality" straight out of the camera. (To be honest, as I look back, it looked nothing like the movies or TV, but it just looked better than HD.) I showed Matt and he loved it. In fact, he loved it so much he started sending it out and booking roles with it. Role after role. He was using it as a reel and not just as a clip submitted to a single casting director. I thought that was genius. Apparently, I was not the only one that thought it was an amazing idea. His girlfriend wanted one. Then her friends wanted one. It was a hit product because it had to be done one time and for a small fee, paid to me, they would be investing in themselves and they would appear more professional in the long run.

Business number two had begun.

One thing led to another and I ended up shooting more videos, for free, in other fields that I was interested in. One time I shot my buddy's GoFundMe pitch video and we walked around New York City capturing B-Roll of him walking around and admiring the city. He was a Brit and he was trying to raise funds to attend the next year at the Academy. This gig was actually paid. Small money, but paid nonetheless. Other friends of his would see that and they asked me to edit their reel, and then Matt asked me to edit his reel once he saw that I knew my way around Premiere Pro.

What I started to learn was that people are lazy and they don't like diving into new things if they don't understand them. For myself, diving into new things and failing, learning from my lessons, and moving forward seemed to come naturally to me. I didn't know it at the time but as I look back, I realize how much I truly enjoy learning new things.

For instance, not to head off track here but I had no idea how to write a book and yet here you are reading my book. That is absolutely insane to me! It's an ongoing thing with me. If someone asked me if I can do something and it interests me, then I try it out.

Long story short, I had another product to sell. I could say I edit actor's reels, take their headshots, and film their monologues or sides for an audition. This was all happening when I was in the middle of creating *Red Soil Productions* with Matthew Stannah and Yudeka Heyer. Since Matt had written his play, as I said, and we were about to put it up Off-Off-Broadway, I had so much to learn.

How do I create a theatre company? How do I create a video production company or a photography company? Should they all be one company? Do I want business partners? Do we have enough money to start one? Where do I go to create one? Can I do it online?

These thoughts and so much more were crossing my mind at the same time, day in and day out. I was trying to figure out how to design posters and tickets. I needed to figure out where and how to rent a theatre for the play. I needed to figure out how to work with the press and an email list. That's when I found out what a "float" was. (The money in the cash box at an event used for change that needs to be handed back to paying customers.)

It was all so much fun and very entertaining. That's not me being sarcastic, I truly loved learning and creating companies. While we were creating, we were asking for money from family members and friends. We came up with a pitch video to ask for funding and sent it to everyone we knew. We made some money with the campaign, but Matt was the one that found the lump sum needed to produce his baby. After I saw how well it worked or didn't work, depending on how you look at it, I shot a pitch video for "tHAt Entertainment." Yup, spelled just like that. I don't know why I used lowercase "t"s in the word "that", but the logo was dope. I felt more professional with a logo. That's when I started branding what was becoming my very own video production company.

15

INVEST IN YOU

I t is tough raising money and finding investors. It's even harder showing a return on that investment. Especially when "investors" for artists are usually family members. The next thing on my list to do was to figure out how to raise money and how to invest in passion projects. This led to some serious soul searching.

When was the last time you invested in yourself? Can you answer that question? Seriously, think about it. It wasn't until the end of 2015 that I learned what investing in one's self actually meant. In fact, those exact words were never even something my ears heard nor had my eyes read.

It was around 8:30 am on a Sunday and I was running down four flights of stairs to take the trash out. In this particular apartment, in Brooklyn, NY, right when you walked into the apartment building there was a little cove to the right, just past the first apartment. In this little cove, there were always little things that people were too lazy to post on Craigslist.

God forbid they would need to walk another 15 feet, through two doors, to throw out what appeared to be trash.

It was rare to find something worth grabbing and lugging up four flights of stairs. People would leave used towels, bowls, lamp shades, pots, pans, mirrors, and whatever they didn't feel like having in their tiny apartment. As soon as something was upgraded, they would remove it from their home and place it right in the hallway under a handwritten sign that read, "FREE." It wasn't pretty to look at when you first walked in because it looked like someone had just won a locker on *Storage Wars*. Every so often, the super or one of the residents would get fed up with the mess and throw it all away.

On this particular day, there was a pile of clothing thrown on the floor. I was on my way down the stairs and the pile was to my left.

I thought, *What a bunch of pigs.*

There were a few trash bags torn apart lying next to the clothes. After sifting through, someone must have been unhappy with the free selection and decided *not* to clean up their mess. I put my trash bag down and started to clean up their mess before it became a tripping hazard. As I moved some of the clothing, I saw a purple book cover. It was rare to find books here and even if I had seen a book, I would have never picked it up. At the time, I thought I was unable to read. Seriously. I'll explain later. It was an attractive color purple and out of the corner of my eye, I saw the word "Dad" written in gold.

I was intrigued. Reason being, for the last month or so, I was trying to have a conversation with my friends about what I had learned from my girlfriend's father. Her family wasn't super rich but they were better off than my family when it came to finances.

The word "finance" was never part of my vocabulary until I had gone on a few trips with my girlfriend's family. As soon as we started planning these trips, I noticed they looked at vacations differently than I had. They looked at borrowing money in a similar way to their vacations. They would throw the word "leverage" around.

Whatever that means!

Credit cards, interest rates, tips, rental properties, automated income, savings, and investing were all topics of conversation right at the dinner table. They never looked down on me but instead educated me when I wanted to learn or when I seemed lost in conversation.

These are definitely not things that were discussed at the dinner table in my own home. They were barely discussed at all at my house. If "finances" were brought up, it became a whisper. I knew what a checkbook, savings account, and checking account were, but that was it. I remember telling my girlfriend to tell her mother and father that I didn't have enough money to fly to the United Kingdom right in the middle of planning our Christmas vacation.

She informed them and they said, "Can he borrow money from his parents and just pay them back after the trip?"

I thought to myself, *No! Fuck NO! Whose parents have a couple of thousand dollars just laying around for their son to go to Wales?*

Clearly, some parents do but I didn't know any. It was almost as if I was from another world and I was seeing this new world for the very first time. I swear, it was the weirdest thing.

When attempting to chat with my buddies about what I had learned, they didn't understand. Looking back, my understanding of money wasn't exactly enough to teach it but I felt like I knew something that all my friends would benefit from knowing. It didn't seem right to hold back this kind of knowledge. The conversations would die quickly when I appeared to be speaking another language in front of them. I felt alone and out of place.

Her parents ended up paying for my flights and hotel rooms on several occasions and I owe them more than I can tell you. Without them, I would have never traveled outside of the United States. Traveling outside of their home country was a usual thing for their family. I just couldn't understand. I couldn't understand why their daughter, my girlfriend at the time, was able to sit on a couch and watch television all day, every day, for as long as she desired and not have to worry about paying rent at the end of every month.

There I was, learning how to strip, trying to sell clothes, and building sets as well as trying to become a professional filmmaker and photographer and she didn't have to work.

How? I wondered.

As you might imagine, I became extremely frustrated and fascinated at the same time. Soon, I found out, through hours of conversations, that her family owned some property and the rental income from the property was enough to cover the mortgage in addition to fully covering her side of the rent in New York City.

I thought, *Wait! What?*

I was so lost. Was I supposed to be upset with the way I was raised? Was I supposed to hate the fact that my parents and their parents were never taught this language of money? How could I be upset? Since it wasn't their fault, *I* decided to take the blame for not understanding how to make and save *my* money. It was now *my* responsibility to understand all there was to know about building wealth and how to use it properly. Especially if I wanted to produce "million dollar movies." If I could figure it out, then there would be no way my future family would have an issue financially. That's the goal, right? The goal is to have your friends and family succeed in ways you never did. After countless attempts to school my friends, I thought I was going crazy.

How do I explain to poor people, that there are ways to not be poor, while I'm not financially stable myself? How do I find out more of what rich people know? What can I do to change my future? How are there people that are able to pay $30,000 per month, on rent alone, in New York City and I can't get a $30,000 salary job?

Someone knew something I didn't and I was determined to figure out what it was. *That* is exactly when I found this purple book with gold lettering. As I removed the rest of the clothes, the purple book that said "Dad," was underneath another book. I bumped the book on top to reveal the words, "Rich Dad."

What? This is insane. It's been on my mind for weeks, if not months at this point, I thought.

I moved the book out from under the pile and the title reads, *"Rich Dad, Poor Dad by Robert Kiyosaki."*

Now, you tell me why this just appeared in my life as soon as I started asking the same exact questions.

Did this book have the answers I was looking for?

Up until that moment in late 2015, I hadn't read a book since 2008. No joke. I graduated high school in 2008 and I never looked back. I watched a lot of movies and Youtube videos but reading would put me to sleep. Back in high school, we had summer reading and nobody wanted to do it. I'll be honest, I cheated on the tests and used SparkNotes quite often.

My mother would say, "Isaac, all you have to do is read a few pages before bed each night and you'll finish it in no time."

Easy for her to say, she can read the entire series of Harry Potter in an hour. That's a bit of an exaggeration and a trait directly delivered via Mom's genes. I never got the reading trait, that's for sure. I would try to read before bed, like a good son and a wonderful student, however, the lines, the left to right, the eyelids, and then Mom waking me up for school the next morning just didn't seem to work out. I thought I just couldn't read. I accepted the fact that books bored me and at the same time, they hypnotized me. I'd fall asleep ten minutes into a book.

I grabbed this *Rich Dad Poor Dad* book, started to run up the stairs, and realized I still needed to throw the trash away. I was so excited I almost forgot. After throwing the garbage out, I raced up the stairs, sat on the couch and opened up the book. My girlfriend and I had been dating for about three and a half years at that point and she never saw me hold a book in my hands once. She would just laugh when I told her how all this new wealth conversation was so intriguing to me because it wasn't anything new to her. She was on her way out the door to go to work, which was a change of pace and a turn of the table. (She was forced to get a job when she had to pay for her VISA. The rental property didn't cover that.) *I* was now sitting on the couch and *she* was off to work on a Sunday.

She asked, "What is that?"

I said, "I don't know. Just found it downstairs. See you when you get back."

She laughed at me as she walked out because it was quite a sight to see.

If I removed myself from my body and put myself in her shoes, *Who is this new boyfriend on my couch? Why is he holding a book?*

It was just as confusing for me but for the first time in my life, I was actually interested in the material I was reading. Let me repeat that because it's very important to understand:

I was very interested in the material I was reading!

For the first time, I didn't feel like it was a chore or something that had to be done. I was reading for myself, to better my future. It felt like an obvious choice. Seventy pages later, my girlfriend returns from work and I'm still on the couch. I love the role reversal here.

Still buried in the book but having to entertain the interruption, I said, "I just found out what 'assets' and 'liabilities' are."

"That's great," taken back by me still reading, "What are you doing?"

"I'm reading. This book is amazing. Remember how I told you this money thing has been on my mind non-stop since the conversation with your dad? Well, this book explains my thoughts perfectly. I'm gonna be rich!"

Confused at how I was, all of a sudden, magically going to be wealthy, she said, "That's good."

Looking back, I probably should have asked how her day

was but I was so involved in the book it actually pissed me off that she was home. Let me put it this way, I had never read more than ten pages in a row in my life and here I was in the seventies, just flipping through. Eyes wide open, no yawning, no complaints, and the best bit: no test at the end. I was in heaven.

That's the moment I learned something extremely important about myself. I thoroughly enjoyed learning about things that interested me. I was so invested in this book that I started to take notes, fold pages where the diagrams were, and I began creating spreadsheets on my computer to track my assets and liabilities. From then on, those two words were glued to my brain every time I went to purchase something.

Will this cost me money or will it make me money in the future?

That thought crossed my mind constantly. I would dream about this new information and come up with ways to acquire money in addition to my consistent income stream.

The other phrase that stuck in my head was, "Pay yourself first!" Robert Kiyosaki kept saying that. After drilling it into my head, I had to try and fully understand what he meant by it.

Then it clicked in my head. I decided to come up with my own unique, money saving, formula inspired by what I had just read. Something that would fit my specific living situation.

What happens when you get paid? Before you even receive your check, you lose hard earned money. Whether or not you get taxes taken out on payday or not, at some point, you owe the government money. For good reasons. I don't want to go into detail about taxes and why we need them or don't need them. All

I'm saying is that right off that bat, you get a massive chunk of change removed from your pocket before you even have control of it. Never mind all the Medicaid and insurances you assume you need to pay for, weekly.

After the money is in your account you have to pay for your car insurance, electricity, hot water, cell phone bills, internet, cable, Netflix, Spotify, gym memberships, groceries, gas, gasoline for your car, maybe a subway pass if you're in a city, and so much more. By the time you pay all these on time, what are *YOU* left with? *NOTHING!!!* That's right, nothing.

Who has *your* money? Everyone but *you*. Why? Why are they making the rules on when you should pay for their service? It took me a second to figure all this out but eventually, I came to the conclusion that putting a percentage of money aside, immediately after I got paid, would be the best way to save my money. Essentially, I would make all my bills wait.

"What? Isaac, there are fees if you don't pay! What is wrong with you?"

That was my way of thinking at first as well. It's okay, you're not alone. Here is my new way of thinking, are you ready?

Here's what I did: I went to my employer and asked him how I could directly deposit my check into my account. This way, I wouldn't have to spend the rest of my Friday in line at a bank along with all the other silly fools depositing checks. I would save time, which is part of understanding your worth and I would save my legs from having to peddle 20 blocks to the bank. I knew this was possible because I had done it at my job before I left for New York City. I remember Thursday evenings, at 11:59 pm, I would get so excited to watch my account jump up a little bit at 12 am on Friday morning. It felt like magic and I had the opportunity again as I was working for another big company with an accountant in the office. At this time I was lucky enough to be offered a job managing a few bars in Brooklyn and I was making $50,000 per year at that job.

Woah! Big Money!

They gave me a paper to fill out and hand back. I took care of that in about three seconds and Voilà. Next week I wouldn't have to race to the bank to skip that line.

"Okay, Isaac, but how the fuck is this helping me save money?"

Well, you little shit, this is how. By depositing money magically into your account, you have one less thing to stress about. To be honest, I'd forget that I had money in my account because I wasn't physically signing the back of the check and handing it over to the bank. I soon became tech-savvy and found out that I could check my balance through the bank's app. That was awesome. The "old me" would have checked the balance and thought that's the amount of money I had to spend. The "new me" saw the balance and didn't want anyone to touch it.

I decided to open up another account, in hopes of being able to transfer my money seamlessly to the second account. That second account would *never* be linked up to the famous "Automatic Payment" option for any of my bills ever again. If I could get paid and instantly transfer as much money as I could to the other account, that would be perfect. Then it dawned on me that I could go *back* to my employer and ask him to deposit all my income into the second account that none of my billing companies knew about. I'll admit, it felt sneaky. By doing this, I would fully control where my money was at all times. At ALL times. It's *my* money. Why would I want anyone else to have it? Then I decided to open up another account.

"Why do you have three accounts now? For what?"

Stop! I'll tell you. As long as you understand that this method is not for everyone. It was specific to my situation at the time. It allowed me to gain control of my money for the first time. It allowed me to start paying things off in the exact order I wanted things paid off. It also allowed me to save. Here we go:

Account 1, will have zero dollars in it until I deposit the money from Account 2. That's right, my bills would now be on hold until I paid them.

They are not stealing my money before I can buy food to eat. It's just not going to happen, sorry!

Account 3 was ONLY to save. I would ask my employer once again to give me a direct deposit slip.

"He's not going to do that, dude."

Want to bet? How about making your employer work for you, for once? Ever thought of that? What's the worst that can happen when you ask?

They say, "No! You've already done this."

You kiss ass and say, "I know, sorry. I messed up the amounts and I'm having a hard time paying bills. It's either that or a raise." Wink at him and see what happens.

"Fine! Here," They'll say.

Now, you have three bank accounts. You with me? On the deposit slip, split the income you are depositing and send it magically to two different accounts. Some people say 80% for your bills and 20% towards your savings and your future. I say, the more the better for your future. If you can afford to put 30-40% away, go for it. The point is *not* how much each time, it's the consistency. After going over how much I was making each week, I could estimate how much I needed to set aside for bills each week--if I intended to pay them at all.

At the time, I was working for a company in Brooklyn that managed bars and my yearly salary was $50,000. It seems like a lot, I know. The rules still apply when you are making $20,000 per year. Trust me, it may just take you longer to save and invest in yourself. That's the only difference. By using this method, I was able to put aside $1,000 every month. With additional sources of income, I was able to save $12,000 in just 6 months. By additional sources of income, I mean picking up odd jobs here and there and working overtime when it was available. Plus any of the filmmaking or photography gigs that paid me.

You might be thinking, *"Okay, but I make $20,000 every year and I can't afford to pay my bills, Isaac."*

You can't pay your bills because you aren't paying yourself first. When you pay yourself first, before your bills, for some reason you spend less on stupid shit and actually use the remainder of your income to pay your bills. I know it sounds backward but it's true.

Think about it, when you see $200.00 in your account, your first thought is either, *"Aw, fuck yeah! We're about to party this weekend,"* or *"Shit, I have groceries, a car payment and my cell phone bill due. How am I supposed to pay all of this with $200.00?"*

You know that you only have $200.00 to spend, so you can either spend it wisely or foolishly. If you want to go blow your hard earned money from the job you despise, great, go for it!

Who's stopping you? If you want to worry about how to pay all of your bills with $200, you can do that as well. Or, you ready for this? Figure out how to make more money to pay your bills.

Here's the other thing, you're looking at Account 1 and its balance says $200.00, so you budget around that. If it said $400.00, you'd budget around that. Maybe you'd pay your bills and party. Good for you, but wouldn't it be cool if Account 1 had a balance of $0.00 in it, Account 2 had a whopping balance of $200.00, and you forgot that you had a third account off in the distance just racking up the balance every week? This only happens if you don't touch it. I don't even want to give Account 3 a balance in this example because I know you will want to spend it. You can't do that. If you want a different lifestyle, as I did, you must do what everyone else around you is *NOT* doing, in order to make that happen. Why stay on the same path when you don't have to? It doesn't make any sense.

Let's do some math. For this example, you are making $300.00 every week. This times 52 weeks in a year will give you a salary job that pays $15,600. Now, let's say that you deposit 66% of your income each month to Account 2. Then you deposit 33% of your income each month to Account 3. Just to clarify, 33% of your income, in this situation, is roughly $100.00 per week. If you are in a month with four weeks in it, by the end of that month you will definitely have $396.00 in Account number 3.

SEE CHART ON NEXT OPAGE

YOUR MONTHLY INCOME		
$1,200		

	66%	33%
ACCOUNT #1 Bills & Spending Only	**ACCOUNT #2** Safe Place	**ACCOUNT #3** Self-Investment
$0	**$804**	**$396**

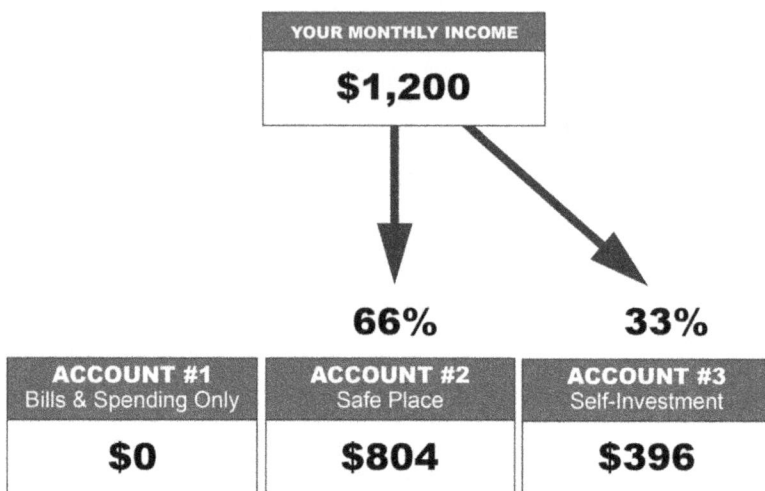

That is assuming you don't touch it, which I forbid you to do until you are ready to invest in your future. If you touch it and spend it, on stupid shit and not on yourself and your future, you'll remain poor and you will never become anything in life. It's a harsh thing to hear, but it's true! I know that sounds really mean but if you want change, you have to be willing to change. It's simple. I know this doesn't sound realistic because you have bills and maybe 33% of your income is too much to put aside at the moment. To be quite honest, it doesn't matter what you are putting aside as long as you are thinking like this and putting at least some money aside for you and your future. YOU! The only person working for that money. *You* deserve it. All of it.

We will use Account 2 to send funds to Account 1 when the bills are due and that will keep you from getting late fees. If you keep doing this, it's simple math that tells you what your future will look like and how long it will take you to get there.

I hope you followed along. The most important thing is for you to have a goal to hit. How do we come up with that number?

It's easy. Find something that you would love to buy, then think, *Will the money I am about to spend right now, help me make more money than I am about to spend, or will I lose this money forever?*

If you are about to spend money that you will never see again, for example, your bills, then you have to make sure that money is not in the same account as the money that will make you more money. I know it sounds confusing so let me explain.

I was doing this before I even read this book and I didn't know I was doing it. I worked long hours and had three jobs in order to pay all my bills. One week I decided to not pay my student loan and it allowed me to take that $600.00 and buy a camera. The camera was an investment for me. I could make my money back and make an unlimited amount of money after I paid it off. It's not something I was going to use once and blow $600.00. In fact, I can't even begin to tell you how much money I made from that one little $600.00 investment. Actually, I am still making money from it today. I just rented it out to a friend to use for a few days and he paid me $100.00 per day. That's not the first time I rented it to him either. See how fast I made my money back? When you play the numbers game, it's a no brainer. Without showing you invoices and statements and whatnot, I will aim low to be as truthful as I can, but I'll tell you that I have made well over $4,000 with that one camera. It actually allowed me to buy another camera, more professional, for $3,200 about two years later. You can see where investing in myself first paid off and I was able to pay bills as well, but later. Even if there were fees, I was able to cover them without any doubt in the world.

Sometimes you need to follow your gut when it comes to

paying your bills after you have paid yourself first. Let me try and give you a practical example, for your own life. You have a cell phone bill and you have a bill from your internet provider. Nowadays you can make phone calls right from your phone if you are on Wi-Fi, and you can use social media apps to socialize or video chat for potential business opportunities. I would recommend paying your internet bill before your cell phone bill. The phone won't just shut off if the bill is not paid. You can still use it on Wi-Fi and most places have Wi-Fi available now. I've done this on several occasions.

One time, I needed to get to New York City because there was $350.00 waiting for me after I filmed for a client. I was about to get paid but at that moment, I didn't have much money. I needed gas and my cell phone bill needed to be paid, but I didn't have enough money to do both. I had to improvise because I needed to use my GPS as well. I opened Google Maps and punched in my destination on Wi-Fi. I proceeded to follow the path Google was showing me and when I hit a gas station, I used my "cell phone bill money" to pay for it. After filling up the car, I made sure to follow the directions exactly as it told me because if I went off course at all I would have been lost without any data. Again, not the end of the world, I could find someone to help me or use someone else's phone to make a call if I needed. After the shoot, I was paid in full via Paypal and used Paypal's debit card to pay for my cell phone bill *and* more gas for the return trip.

These situations are only temporary. They don't last forever, but we tend to stress about these insignificant things way too often and it's unhealthy. Ideally, we just want to be able to pay our bills and be happy at the same time, am I right? I find the only way that works for me is to pay myself first. Every time. By paying yourself first, and following your gut with what gets paid first, you are doing your future self a massive favor. If you have paid yourself first for long enough, when a problem arises, it no longer becomes a problem when money can take care of it. It becomes a hefty expense rather than a stressful week of crying and hating yourself for not putting money aside sooner. Don't think of it as a savings account. Think of it as a Self-Investment account.

I want to discuss a bigger situation where I had to make a very tough decision while forcing myself to create a better future for myself and the people around me. The next chapter has an extreme example of what I've been talking about. I do not recommend that you try this. However, the point of the story is for you to understand that I've also had to make some very tough choices and followed my gut every single time. In the end, everything worked out. It cost me a little more money in the long run but it also bought me so much more time. Time is precious.

Remember, if you know your worth, you will know the value of your time.

16

SIX MONTHS

It was a rough couple of years trying to build my own businesses without investors. I know some people think the only way to build a business is to reach out and find investors, and although that is one way to go about it, I have a serious issue with letting people own a percentage of my company, for only handing me money. If I'm the one doing all the work, why should anyone else get a cut, you know what I'm saying? I'm wrestling with this concept that at times, doesn't seem to be very effective. It was only recently that I had enough confidence to raise my prices and charge what I knew my time was worth. Up until that point, I was stretching $150.00 to the moon and back. I literally have no idea how I managed to get to where I am today if my monthly income was averaging $400.00 per month. I could go multiple weeks and stretch $50.00. There was no guarantee that my potential clients would end up paying for my services or if I would even acquire new customers. Some months were slower than others and some makeup for three months. It had been rough and I'm sure you can relate.

Anyways, I received a letter in the mail, from my car insurance company, stating that my six-month policy was coming to an end and it was time to renew it. Since I had no idea where my money was coming from next, I wanted to make sure I spent the money that I had wisely. If I invested the money into paying for my car insurance that would be great but I wouldn't be able to buy groceries. I needed to eat. Right around that time, I had been getting ready for a couple of road trips with a friend of mine, for business.

I thought, *Why would I waste precious money on a car that will not be used while I'm away?*

It's not a great idea for everyone, but *I* chose to let that notice slide. The letter sat on my dresser for a week. Then two. Then three and so on. Three weeks later and three letters later, I received my final notice and a warning about my registration being void in Massachusetts without car insurance.

I said, "Cool," and I threw that letter away.

I hate being told what to do and I wanted to see how long I could get away with spending my money on shit that would make me money faster.

You're probably thinking, *"Wouldn't his car get him to New York and back to make good money?"*

Why, yes it would. That's a great point. My rebuttal would be that I just so happened to be going through a learning phase and schooled myself on how to make money online in late 2015. I was also teaching myself how to raise money for new film projects. You'll learn more about why I decided to give up my cushy $50,000 per year, full-time job in the following chapters.

For a year and a half, I spent most of my waking hours investing in courses, books, and filmmaking equipment. I guess you could say I was paying tuition in a weird way. Not to a school but to masters of their craft. In the online world, it becomes very costly because the return on one's investment is so massive and the gurus understand the value of their products. At the same time, I had no need to leave the house and I still don't as I am writing this book. If I did leave, it was for groceries and the supermarket is down a few back roads and nowhere near the police.

Course after course, page after page, video after video, I finally figured it out. It was time to get back to marketing and experimenting with what I had just learned. Time to put it into action and find out for myself. It failed. Every time. Why? I had to learn how to design websites, landing pages and pay for ads. It was a never-ending cycle of just spending money, learning, and applying. Something just kept telling me to keep learning. I can't explain everything I learned about online marketing. There are too many different opinions and techniques to add it to this book. Along the way, I learned pricing strategies. I learned sales. I learned how to talk to clients. I'm telling you, I maxed out all my credit cards and solely focused on learning how to make money and a lot of it. I studied automated income and how to publish books, like this one. Learning how to use my own story as my product was a game changer. I wanted to learn everything I could and figure out the best way to produce more movies and web-series. It would help me get new eyes on my content.

My mailbox was full of subtle reminders along with my inbox. Now they were emailing me and telling me I *had* to do this and that "OR ELSE."

Woopty fuckin' doo.

I wasn't scared. What's the worst that could happen? I played out all the scenarios in my head. The worst one was, *I'm sitting in a jail cell with positive energy and I'm making friends with bigger dudes than me.*

No, really, I wasn't going to go to prison when all I was doing was sitting at my desk all day and my car was sitting in the driveway. It wasn't harming anyone. It wasn't driving through town at 70mph. In all honesty, I was a bit scared to drive to the gym a couple of miles away. I was worried I was going to get caught.

Although this thought kept crossing my mind, I became ballsier and ballsier over time. I received a letter from the state of Mass explaining that my registration was no longer valid and I had to pay $100.00 to renew it. I didn't have $100.00 at the time. Guess what I did? I ignored that too and continued paying for food and that was about it. I even stopped paying my cell phone bill and only used that damn thing on Wi-Fi. If I tell you how to live your life, it's because I've already gone through this bullshit and want to help you get through it when it's your turn. The time will come. It always does. The question is, when will the time arrive?

I practiced my "getting pulled over" speech in my head a dozen times. By now, I had booked a couple of filming gigs in New Hampshire and some in New York City. How was I going to get there without a car from Massachusetts?

You might be thinking, *"Why are you living in MA?"*

I couldn't afford NYC anymore after quitting my job and leaving my girlfriend. More on this later.

Anyways, I couldn't get paid without a car. I had some

thinking to do. Either I never take the gig and stress myself out even more about where my income was coming from or I just drive like a normal human being and drive safely. That's what I did.

I hopped in my car and started driving to New York City. Let's put it this way, I couldn't pay for tolls either. Just gas to get there and food when I was there. These are the things I never thought twice about paying for when I was making a decent wage at a company, but when I had a hard time purchasing hot dogs and ramen noodles, I had to take risks on another level. It was scary. Every time I hopped in my truck I had to sidetrack my mind from the negative thought of getting pulled over by listening to podcasts and audiobooks. I knew that if I thought about getting pulled over before I had the money to actually pay for the fines and renewals, I would stress out even more than I was already. The idea was to just keep driving and driving safely.

I kept telling myself this throughout the entire drive, *Don't speed! Don't tail! Keep your eyes open!*

I was able to drive there and back and wherever else and back too. I was booking small little gigs that would pay a couple of hundred dollars but nothing crazy. That was my income. One time, I even tried to pay for insurance for a month because I had put enough aside to pay for one month's worth. It wasn't worth it and I couldn't pay the next month when it was due again. I decided I was going to wait to book a solid gig, that paid a decent amount, to pay off six months up front and then renew my registration. I wasn't able to put money aside because I wasn't making any during this phase.

I booked a wedding gig in New Hampshire and the photographer I was working with said he was going to drive. All

I had to do was meet him at the studio, and we'd go from there. He drove all the way up and all the way back. By the time we got back, it was about 12:30 am and I had to drive home. It wasn't a long drive, only twenty-five minutes or so. Until that point, I refrained from driving at night because, where I lived in MA, there are less civilians on the road than cops. They've got nothing better to do than run your plate or pray that you have a tail light out.

What's that phrase, *Nothing good happens after 11 pm?*

I could never remember the time in that phrase but I kept moving it closer and closer to sunset. Nothing good was going to happen to *me* as soon as that sun set.

I packed up my car with the equipment from the shoot and started heading home. As I pulled out, I saw a cop just sitting on the main street, watching and waiting to have a good time. Either I would have to wait there until he relocated or I would take my chances and drive like a normal person. I was tired and I wasn't about to wait for him to relocate so I took a left and crossed his field of view.

Fwew, I got away with it. Wait...fuck, not a red light.

Bam. I had to stop at the red light, obviously. It felt like the longest light ever. Green means go so I lightly pushed that skinny little pedal on the right to get away from the officer. About a mile down the road, I looked in my rear view mirror and it was pitch black.

SCORE!

I was as free as a bird until I blinked and there were two headlights racing up behind me.

Oh shit, he's got a call. Let me pull over, I thought.

Dumbass.

I pulled over to let him pass and he pulled in right behind me. I grabbed my license and registration that appeared to be in date still, turned the light on, and sat there. I rolled my window down and I heard my full name in a deep ass voice coming up on my left.

"Isaac Danna! Isaac Danna!"

Who the fuck is this guy?

That's never happened to me before. Out of all the times I've gotten pulled over, they never say your name before you show them your license and registration. It was odd. I felt set up. I turned my head and I saw someone I recognized.

"What's going on with the insurance?" He said.

"Hey, man! How the hell have you been," I said, "What do you mean? I have insurance. I just renewed it."

It wasn't a complete lie because I did just buy that one month of insurance but the registration was still not linked to the new insurance because after it ran out, it started the process over again.

"It says your registration is invalid and you do not have insurance."

I tried to white lie my way out of it, "Oh shit. Sorry, dude. I literally just paid for it. I'll sort it out."

"It's good to see you, Isaac. I saw your name when I ran the plates and I wanted to make sure you were aware of the situation. Get it fixed."

"Thank you!"

The officer started walking away, turned and said, "Oh, Isaac?"

"What's up?"

"This conversation never happened! Got it?"

"Got it! Thanks. Have a nice night!"

"You too!"

That was too close for comfort and just the beginning of this little journey of mine.

~

One afternoon I was out behind my aunt and uncle's house as an older gentleman walked around the side of their house and into their backyard. He said, "I think I backed into someone's car when I was backing my horse trailer out of the street."

My grandparents had just come up from Florida to visit for a little while and they were also hanging out there along with my mother and father. We were just going to have a little BBQ and enjoy each other's company and this guy interrupts with wonderful news.

We all walked around to the front of the house and he pointed to my truck that was parked, legally, on the side of the street and said, "That's the one I think I hit."

Making sure I hear him correctly, "You think you hit? How are you not sure?"

He didn't answer me. We walked over to the driver's side of my truck and he pointed out a significant dent in my rear driver door.

He asked, "Was that there?"

"Nope! This little scrape was but definitely not the dent you just made."

My whole family was fucking heated, but I was keeping my composure. They were all so infuriated and couldn't understand why I wasn't knocking this guy's lights out. For one, I hate confrontation that doesn't end with desirable results. Most altercations end up worse when you approach them with anger or hostility. For two, I was the only one that knew I had no insurance or registration at the time.

"Let me back my truck up and see if it really was me. I want to see if it matches up, you know?" The guy was just trying to make sure he was at fault.

"Fine."

I looked at my family, who was now enraged and yelling, "Woah! Woah! Woah! Stop!"

The guy almost rear-ended my vehicle, again. I almost died laughing because I was looking at this situation differently from the others that had made this *their* business.

I told my father, grandfather, and uncle, "I got this, thank you. I got this. We'll figure it out. I'll deal with it," and I pointed to the back yard.

Like puppies getting yelled at, they walked away and kept turning their heads back to make sure I had full control of the situation. Family, eh? Always got your back.

The guy got out of his truck and said, "Thank you. I don't mind dealing with you. You're the only sensible one here. They're all drunk!"

This was said just as he walked over to his passenger side and opened the door to reveal a couple of O'Doul's in the seat. "They're non-alcoholic!" he said, faster than it took my eyes to see them.

He grabbed a piece of paper, "Let's exchange information and see if we can't settle this without a police report."

I said, "Great idea."

"Unless you want me to call the police and we can square it away now and fill them in on what happened."

He started for his phone and I said, "No! Wait! I think we can handle this. I'll get a quote for you and we can go from there. No need to involve the cops and shit, you know? I think we have this under control."

If those cops were called, my driving days were over. Obviously, I would have to suck up a dent in my door but I wasn't too concerned. The door still opened and the windows rolled up and down. A dented door, or no car for who knows how long? Exactly. We exchanged information and went our separate ways.

A few days later, I got a quote and called him, "It's going to be almost $2,000."

Not pleased with my quote, "Nevermind, I can't afford that right now. I'll file a claim with my insurance company."

Two days later, I received a phone call from his insurance company and they were ready to file a claim after I gave them my side of the story. They began a file and asked me to drive to their location for an inspection. I asked them if I needed to bring my insurance paperwork and they said no. I was in the clear because he was 100% at fault. The inspection went as expected and they informed me that a check would be sent out immediately and that I could use the check however I pleased because it was in my name. Seeing how I had a few projects that needed to be finished and I needed to eat, I was looking forward to using that money. (Plus, at this point, I had to pay a few family members back because I borrowed a couple of hundred dollars even though I didn't want to. Again, family! Got to love them.) So this check was going to pay off my small debt to the family, pay for food, get my Wake Up Masterclass hosted online and hopefully after that, pay for my insurance again. I swear that was the plan. I know it sounds backward.

I drove my uninsured and unregistered vehicle to *his* insurance company for the inspection. On my way back from the inspection, I remembered telling my mom the night before that I was going to stop by the next day to help with a piece of technology she was having a hard time with. She wasn't home when I arrived and I started to head back to my Brother's Girlfriend's Mother's house to get some work done in the basement.

At the top of their dirt road, I turned left and I heard a massive bang. I thought I was about to die, it was so loud. I kept driving until I could safely pull over up head. Either I had a flat or something fell off under the car and it was now dragging. I couldn't tell you. I pulled over, turned the car off, and took a peek underneath. Let's just say it wasn't pretty and I know nothing about cars. There was a moment where I wished I'd spent all that time and money learning how to become a mechanic instead. The muffler appeared to be broken, half on the ground and half hanging on for dear life. Seriously.

"You okay, man?"

There was a voice coming from behind me. I heard footsteps and I turned around to see a young man, my age, coming over to help. He dove under the car as he said, "Let me take a look."

I backed off and let this guy do his thing. "Do you have any wire in the car," he asked.

Flustered, "I don't think so. Let me..."

"How about a metal coat hanger?"

I knew I definitely didn't have that but my parents might

have one. I said, "I'll be right back. I'm going to run down to my parent's house and see if they have one."

"I can drive you! I don't mind."

Okay, who the hell is this guy? Why is he helping me?

He drove me down to my parent's and back up to the car. This guy says, "I got this," and dove under the car again. He bent the coat hanger around a hook that was still intact. Then proceeded to wrap the coat hanger around the muffler and hung it as close as he could to where it broke off. It was magical. Simply magical. I would have never thought about doing that and the only reason he knew how to do it was because one of his buddies just had the same exact thing happen to him. What are the odds?

It was fixed. Sort of. I couldn't thank him enough and asked him for his number in case *he* needed a hand at some point. After the exchange and a massive showcase of gratitude, I drove nice and slowly back to the house.

The next day, I took a trip to my mechanic and asked him what the damage would be. It wasn't as bad as I thought but still costly. There goes the rest of that fat check I was waiting on.

Damn it!

The great thing about this little dilemma was that if this happened before the accident, all of this money would have come out of my own pocket to fix this. Now, it was as if the dude that hit my car was paying for the whole thing. That was a lovely feeling. It's all about how you look at it.

The hard truth is, once again, I was unable to pay for insurance. Especially after his insurance company sent the check to my old address assuming I still lived there. It took three weeks before I found it in my mailbox after they resolved the issue. By then, whatever money I had was spent on food. The leftover money from the check, if any, was used for food and business cards for an expo I was about to be a part of. Guess how I got there? You guessed it. My uninsured vehicle. Man, you're getting good at this game.

At the expo, I networked with a ton of people and had a bunch of leads for video production and photography. Earlier I mentioned how I raised my prices, mid expo, to see what people would say and one of the guys really liked my work. Enough to not care about price. He ended up hiring me for $1,500.

"What? That's amazing."

Another person was planning on hiring me for a $500 gig. Now I'd have plenty of money to pay for six months of insurance. This time, I was going to make it a priority. I set up the $1,500 shoot first and squared away all the details. Since I had never gotten paid that much in my life for a shoot like that, I couldn't wait. I asked my friend Brittany to assist to make it look like I was a bigger deal than I was. It worked. You always look like you know what you are doing if you have a helper or a personal assistant working with you.

The shoot was an hour and a half away from where I lived. It wasn't three hours away like some of New York City shoots that paid less. Time aside, I was driving illegally. We arrived at the shoot and it lasted no longer than three and a half hours so we packed up as fast as we could and headed off once again, but not before collecting the full payment. My client wrote a check and smiled as he gave it to me. He knew the photos we had captured that day were amazing so he had no problem dishing out my payment.

An hour and twenty minutes later, the sun had set and

Brittany and I were enjoying the purplish hue in the sky. This shoot ended fairly early and I was trying to get back to my house before it got dark.

Those coppers, man!

We had music blasting while driving the speed limit, obviously. Very aware of the police cars setting speed traps along the way, I drove very carefully that evening. I approached a red light and started to slow down just as it turned green. (I hate when that happens. The red light has been lit up for a minute at the intersection and you're preparing to stop and wait for a minute. Then, Bam! The light changes to green, after your car and your entire body, have accepted a complete stop. At that moment, I am enraged for all of about one second until embracing the fact that I get a chance to gas it and avoid holding up all the traffic behind me.)

As I was stopping at the red light, there was a cop up ahead. No more than one hundred yards away.

As if I didn't see him. Lights shut off. Parked. Dark colored vehicle.

Come on! I found you, Bro! Let's play.

The light changed to green and I stepped on it. Nothing too crazy but enough to get me up the hill I was approaching. Once again, the police car vanished into the distance. I wish I was keeping a tally of how many times I was able to pass a cop without getting my plates run through the system.

Damn! I really should have done that just for this book. How cool would that have been? Sorry.

I drove for another three minutes or so, and then I had to stop at another light to turn left. My house was less than seven minutes away from this particular light. I was on Route 20, turning left onto Route 31. You can see the intersection from a quarter mile away. There are Jersey barriers dividing the east and westbound traffic from colliding into one another.

For the last three minutes, that barrier was to my left the entire way down to this light. You physically cannot take a left until this light and there is even a turn-out at the light, for people who want to spin around and head back east. I say this because I saw a cop on the other side of the street and I was watching him to see if he was parked or pulling out of the parking lot up ahead. In the parking lot he was in, there were only two ways to leave the lot. You could either leave and head east on Route 20 or exit on Route 31 which would land him on the exact street I was about to take a left on. I wanted to make sure he wasn't going to turn onto 31 and if he did, I would drive slow enough for him to be in front of me.

I stopped at the red light and waited for my turn to go left. I kept looking to my left to see where he was. He was backing out of the parking spot and I had no idea where he was going. I checked my mirror on the passenger side to see if there was anyone next to me or if anyone was coming up behind me. If there wasn't, I was going to switch lanes, last minute, and avoid this situation altogether but there was someone to the right and some headlights behind me as well. When I noticed the headlights behind me, I saw the silhouette of what appeared to be an emergency light bar on top of the truck. I only saw it because there was another car pulling in behind the truck that had pulled up behind me. As soon as I saw the light bar, it turned on and flashed blue and red right in my eyes.

There was no time to process or avoid this. I swear this cop dropped out of the clouds. As I was saying, I saw one further back but he stayed put at the last intersection. To this day, I still think he just fell behind me. It's either that or I totally missed the crane gently placing him behind my uninsured and unregistered vehicle. Just to top it off, I had noticed at that moment that my inspection sticker was no good either. By one month.

This should be fun.

I turned left and prayed that if there was a God, he'd let the officer pass me and head to the emergency call down the road. Since there is no God, there was no emergency call. The beautiful lights were accompanied by a brief wave recognized as a siren and I was encouraged to pull over my 2004 Ford Escape.

Brittany asked, "What's going on?" as she snapped back to reality after being buried in her phone for the last thirty minutes.

"Nothing! I just got pulled over. He just ran my plates."

She knew what that meant because I told her prior to our trip what was going on. She was actually more upset than I was, because I knew this was going to happen at some point and when better for it to take place than right now, with a $1,500 check in my pocket? I couldn't think of a better time. In fact, once I realized that I had that check in my pocket, I laughed and smiled as I reached into the glove box and grabbed my registration that was never going to work. The officer approached the vehicle on the driver's side.

$\sim$

"Why did you say the driver's side? That's obvious."

You know, I used to think the same thing until I got pulled over for a tail light out one time and the cop just blinded me with the spotlight on the driver's side and ended up knocking on the passenger side window.

I rolled the window down and said, "You got me! I thought you would be on this side," and laughed.

"That's why I came to this window," he said, with the best shit-eating grin I've ever seen.

He let me go after we discussed that I was just getting out of the movies after watching "Split". Apparently, he wanted to watch it too and hadn't had the chance yet. That's when the situation took a turn for the better as it became more of a movie review than a civil infraction. Anyways, that's why I said, "The driver's side."

~

Once again, I rolled my window down and handed my license and registration, to the cop that had dropped out of the sky, before he could even ask for it. It's pretty ridiculous that I know how all this shit works because I've gotten pulled over so many times. To be honest, because I know how this shit works I seem to get let off more than I get written up. Sometimes there isn't even a warning given to me. I will say, that's where "White Privilege" comes into play. That's not racist. It's fact and I had no choice on what color or ethnicity I wanted to be when I was born. This is a gift that I must not forget and I am giving credit directly to the "Creator" who also pulled me over on this night in history.

"What's going on with the insurance," the cop asked.

Now, I had a choice. *Do I lie and say, "What do you mean? I have insurance..." like all the times I had rehearsed this prior to the day of its arrival? Do I use honesty under these circumstances because honesty is the best policy?*

I decided to use honesty, "I haven't been able to afford it."

"Okay, I'll be right back. I *am* going to have to tow your car and take the plates."

I took a second to process this. *How was I going to get home? Who was I going to call? Where was the car going to end up? How long would it be till I was able to get it back?* The officer went back to his car and started filling out the paperwork.

Then Brittany said, "Ask him if he can follow you home and take the plates when you get there."

Thought in a Manchester, English accent, *FUCKING GENIUS, she is.*

I poked my head out the window, even though I was still buckled. All I saw was the blinding light and another police car behind the one that pulled me over. The second officer started joking and laughing with the first one while standing by the original police vehicle. I asked, "Excuse me. Excuse me."

"What's up?"

"Is there any way..." With a gulp in my throat, "...is there any way that you might be able to follow me home and take the plates when I get there? I only live 7 minutes down this street."

There was a second officer who replied, "We can't do that, sorry. If we could, we would."

∽

There are not many things that irk me in life but answers like that really fucking piss me off. There was no explanation as to why they couldn't. It brings me back to my younger years when my father would just tell me "No," and call it a day. I hate being told "No," with no explanation to follow. If there is no explanation, it becomes a way of empowering the person withholding the information. It's simply degrading to the person that needs more information. That's just "the way it is," because you said so? I don't fucking think so! I'm not the kind of guy that likes to be told what to do without explanations on why that is the process. The reason for that, is I tend to have much better ideas, systems, and processes than the person dishing them out. Hence why I have quit every job I've ever had. I solve problems for a living. That's what entrepreneurs do. We learn from being told "No," after being given the reason why the customer doesn't like the product or doesn't want our services.

I digress. The answer was "No," and I wasn't about to get all worked up about it because cops aren't the kind of people that give a fuck what you're plans are, were, or will be. They're the law and we have to respect what they do. So I did.

The tow truck came and this guy was no older than me. Brittany and I are standing on the curb, she's shivering, being a tough chick in the cold, and I am waiting to see what the next right thing to do is. I knew from past experiences that some companies like this took checks. I had a checkbook at the house. I figured I'd give him a check when he dropped us off. Maybe the check would bounce, maybe it wouldn't.

The tow truck driver says, "How's it going?"

I laughed out loud and said, "Aw, it's great. I love when I get my car towed!"

I probably sounded like a dick but from where I'm from, that's just sarcasm. He laughed, so it was all good.

"How will you pay for this," he asked.

"Check!"

"Nope! We don't take checks *and* you have to pay now with cash or credit."

Damn it!!

I was planning on pulling a fast one by handing him a check with numbers on it from an account no longer in use. Checks are such an outdated form of payment. I knew it was illegal but I would have paid the next bill when they finally noticed that the check had bounced. It would have just bought me more time while having to deposit this check.

Luckily, I had forgotten that I had a couple of hundred dollars in my checking account already because I had raised my prices recently. How great is that? Again, if money can solve a problem, it's not a problem. I believe Warren Buffet said that. Don't quote me on it.

There I was, about to get towed and not a care in the world. The cop walked over with a slip. He handed it to me and said, "I waived the fine. You can fight this in court if you drop this off in the next 4 days. It's up to you."

"Wonderful! Thanks," I replied.

I didn't look at it and put it in my pocket. Britt and I hopped up in the tow truck as the guy finished strapping my Escape to the bed. I will say, he was rather rough with my baby. I bought this Escape with cash. I have no payments because I invested in myself and bought it outright. It was $2,500 with 90,000 miles on it. Some girl was selling it in Brooklyn, NY because she came from Connecticut and hated alternate side parking rules in the city. I took it off her hands and it was a great deal. I've put a lot of money into it with tires, breaks, and some other car things I don't understand but it runs wonderfully. All and all, I wanted to make sure he wasn't ruining my baby. There were so many straps around my tires and the undercarriage that I was rather impressed. It looked like he actually wanted my truck to survive. However, I did notice that he cranked the straps so tightly around my tires that the rubber started molding around the strap. Thank God it never happened, but I wondered if he would have to purchase new tires if he popped them. That's what I was nervous about.

He drove us back to my house and dropped the truck off in the driveway, after manually filling out a service form and receipt. The whole process seemed very outdated but there I was, my car was safe and sound. I couldn't drive it without the plates, obviously, but it was home. I forgot to say that the cop actually came over to my car and unscrewed my plates off while I was still in it. Before he handed me the slip. He told me that if I had all the required paperwork in order, in the next few days, I would be able to pick up my plates at the police station because he would hold onto them for me.

The worst was over. I just went inside and went to bed. I lied, I ate dinner and then went to bed. It's the best thing to do, really. It's really healthy for you. (Insert winky face emoji here.) It really wasn't a big deal to me because I knew this was going to happen at some point. So far, it was actually better than I thought. The cop allowed me to tow my car to my house instead of the garage. That saved me a few dollars. I would have had to pay the "gate fee," per day if it was impounded. So I was already stoked at how this played out. I just didn't know what else I could do that evening since it was now 9 pm on a Saturday. The banks would be closed on Sunday.

Also, since I had been depositing checks that were anywhere

from $300 to $800, I had learned from experience that a check larger than my average deposit would take a few more days to verify. So I wouldn't have the full insurance payment until Wednesday of the next week, at the very earliest.

Do I stress about it for the next few days or do I just accept the fact that I have to borrow a roommate's car if I really, really, needed to go somewhere?

Why stress? It would all be figured out at some point. I did everything in my power to get it sorted as fast as I could.

On Monday, I deposited the check via the bank's app so I didn't even need to leave the house. I used the rest of the day to write a few pages in this book. Tuesday morning, at 12 am, I checked my balance to see, just for shits and giggles, how much money was deposited. It was all there.

YAY!

See what happens when you just do the right thing and stay positive? I don't know how that happened but it was all there. It wasn't a "pending balance" either. It was "available." I couldn't believe my eyes.

I went to bed because, once again, there was nothing I could do at that moment. I asked my brother the night before if I could use his car to make all the trips and get it all squared away in one day. When I woke up the next morning I just felt so motivated to write this book that I waited another day. Wednesday was as good a day as any. However, because I stayed home and wrote the book on Tuesday, I was forced to figure out the best way to write from home. Up until this point, I had been going to the library and grabbing a Dunkin's for my writing sessions. It seemed to work wonders but I could only write three to four pages at a time and then I would crash and my brain would freeze up. I'd leave and say I would head back to the library later for another session but I never did, let's be honest here. So writing from home is amazing, there are no excuses. If I need more coffee, I just make more coffee. I loved it so far. I was able to write more pages every day I wrote from home than at the library. Everything just works out for the best when you are on the right positive wavelength.

Anyways, I knew that one more day wasn't going to hurt me so I wrote for the day and Wednesday was going to be the day I got my car back on the road. Tuesday afternoon I noticed that the paper the cop gave me was actually a criminal complaint against me. That was something I didn't see coming. A criminal offense for not having insurance? That's insane. The law is the law, so I made sure to get my act together and prepared for the next day. I did my research and got all the paperwork organized in a folder that I would take to all the places I had to go on Wednesday.

First thing was first, I needed car insurance and since we have the interweb I could acquire this car insurance by signing up online and not having to drive anywhere. Clever, huh? Wednesday morning, I ran to my office (built by yours truly) which is in the basement of my youngest Brother's Girlfriend's Mother's house. (It's cheap to rent and I'm able to spend all my days writing this book and being an artist. Judge if you want) Anyways, I ran to my office and applied for insurance with the same company I had before. All my details were already on file so the process was easier than I thought it would be. *Sweet!* Six hundred dollars later, I had insurance in Mass for six months.

Next on the list was to head to the RMV and renew my registration that was canceled due to having no insurance. I brought all my paperwork down to the RMV, including two forms of identification, and was in and out with a brand new registration in less than ten minutes with my pockets $100.00 lighter. I shit you not, these tasks were flying by.

From there, I had to stop at the police station to prove that I had taken care of the issue so he would return my plates like he said he would. Before I left the RMV, the woman behind the counter was not in a lovely mood and she hit me with the negative energy saying, "They usually throw the plates away." She gave me a nasty face and wished me luck. Thinking I'd be back to see her soon, she said, "It's twenty bucks to get new plates."

"Thanks," I said, and left that energy so fast. I trusted the officer who took my plates because he really was a nice guy and in my opinion, he could have punished me more than he had. I *am* thankful for that. How am I getting around you ask? I borrowed Brittany's car, okay? I arrived at the police station and the female officer behind the glass said, with a lovely smile on her face, "How can I help you?" She was so happy compared to the woman I just encountered at the RMV.

I requested that my plates be returned to me and showed her the required paperwork. Three minutes later, I had my plates in my hand. So far, this took all of an hour to complete. After the police station, I continued with my journey and screwed my plates on the front and back of my truck. This moment was amazing, I felt so accomplished. It's weird, even now, knowing I have car insurance when I had been driving around without it for at least 6 months total.

Since I had insurance, a valid registration and my plates were back on my vehicle, it was time to get it inspected. I went to a garage that a friend of mine owned but they were busy so I had to go to another one. That was the only wasted time of that day. The next garage had empty bays and for a small payment of $35.00, I was able to get my sticker.

BOOM!

I was approaching the two-hour mark for time spent on these tasks. Next, I had to drop off that paper at the court no later than that day or else there was a warrant out for my arrest.

Again, really? How is driving without something you are told you need a criminal offense? How about murder? You're telling me they're in the same group? Come on!

It is what it is and I had to sort it out. I showed up at the court and found out that I wasn't going to have to sit in a courtroom, at least this time. I was told that I was going to have a hearing with the Court Magistrate and the officer from the town that wrote the complaint would be present as well. This was great news because I had been in a similar room, earlier in my life, if you recall. No worries.

The time had come, it was time to see the Court Magistrate. I showed up bright and early and explained myself. Once again, honesty was key at that moment. He told me I would need to come back and appear in front of a judge because he didn't have the power to wave this criminal offense. He informed me that it would probably cost no more than $100.00. That pleased me.

I went back to court a month later and spoke with the judge. He asked if I had all my paperwork in order and I showed him my folder. He charged me a $50.00 fee to be paid whenever I could. Since I was prepared for this moment, I had brought my debit card with just over $100.00 on it. I ran downstairs after saying, "Thank you," and paid my fine. I asked the woman when the money would be taken out so I could make sure there were no bounced fees or overdrafts that were taking place. She told me that the money would be taken out in a couple of hours.

～

Christmas came and went but because I had to pay for my car, unfortunately, I couldn't afford Christmas gifts. Then New Years came and went. Over the holidays, I had spoken to a client that I had shot for, just before the new year. He asked me if I wanted to shoot in the first week of January. He was a motivational speaker and his story is amazing. The gig consisted of two shoots in one day and one shoot the next day. I signed up for all three. These shoots were fairly easy to produce so I agreed to $200.00 per shoot because it was about two hours worth of work. The total price came to $600.00 both days.

I woke up bright and early, stopped at Dunkin's to treat myself, and was on my way. About twenty minutes into the drive, I drove past a cop that was on my right side. He was tucked away in between some trees but I still saw him. I felt nervous as I drove by. Something didn't feel right even though everything was taken care of. About a quarter of a mile down the road, I could still see him in my rearview mirror. I flashed my headlights to warn the oncoming traffic that there was an officer camping out ahead of them. It was just then that I saw him pull out and start driving.

I thought, *This can't be right. Did he just see me warn the other cars?*

I used to be quite a punk and I had a reputation for speeding when I was in my teens. In fact, there were a few occasions where the cop was headed the other way and I sped past him. I saw him turn around and I booked it down a couple of side streets and lost him.

However, this time, due to my successes in the past and my recent encounter with the law, I had to make a decision. *Do I turn left here or do I just get pulled over and show him that I am all caught up?*

I actually wanted to pull over, just to prove that I was in the right this time. That's what I did. I pulled over and he did the whole "license and registration," thing, once again.

"Why are you driving an unregistered vehicle?"

Inside, I was so excited. It was my turn to punch back, "It's registered. I just paid for it. Literally, two weeks ago, I was in court and I just paid fifty bucks."

He seemed like he didn't believe me, "Really? Then why is it telling me that your registration has not been renewed due to a bounced check?"

I have no fuckin' idea, officer. You tell me! I paid with a debit card.

Then it hit me! When I originally signed up for my registration the very first time, well before any of this had happened, I had used a check because their card reader wasn't working. I knew that check might bounce and I gave it to the clerk anyways because I had a shoot in New York City that night. I'll take the blame for it but their machine wasn't working and I only had money on a debit card. It wasn't like it was a credit card or anything. I tried to get out of this one by saying that I had no idea, because I just didn't want to believe that was the case. I was literally just in court a few weeks prior and they could have told me that it was no good. In fact, in order for me to get my car back, I had to pay for my registration.

Wouldn't you think the RMV would have said, "Wait a minute, you have an outstanding balance from nine months ago because your check bounced?"

That would make sense, but nope. Not for this situation. The cop was really nice and I could see he felt bad. Either way, he had to do his job. He called the tow company and I called my brother who was on call for the Fire Department the night before. As I'm sitting in the back of the cop car, I told the officer that my brother was on his way and that it took him a second to pick up the phone because he was on call the night before.

He said, "On call? Where?"

I said, "He's a Firefighter, here in town."

"Why didn't you say that right off the bat? I hate paperwork," he said.

"WHY!?"

That made me even angrier. My brother saved me and picked me up after I removed all my filming gear from the back of my car. Time to play this whole game ALL OVER again.

I was fifteen minutes away from my gig that was going to pay me $200.00 and then I had another gig that night for the same wage. Luckily this guy had hired me before and because I showed up early and shot well, he knew I would never just not show up. I texted him and told him that I wasn't going to make it to the shoot that morning. I told him that I would borrow my Brother's Girlfriend's car to get to the second shoot that evening. I asked him to pay me for the evening shoot and the one the next day when I arrived that evening. If he could do that, I would be able to pay for the fee at the RMV, get my plates back, and retrieve my car back from the tow company. He knew I would never blow him off and he knew I wouldn't steal his money and not show up after he paid me. He paid me.

"Jorge, if you read this book, I just want to thank you once again."

The next day, I used the entire payment of $400.00 to pay fees and any charges to get my car back. I also dropped off the second criminal summons I received in two months. I knew how that whole process worked (a little too well) at this point. They told me to wait for a hearing again and that's where I'm at now. This just happened a few weeks ago. I can assume that the same thing will happen and if I plan for the worst, I will have to pay another $100.00 to the court. That's okay. I have the money now. I finally caught up and I did it without working for the "The Man" or "The Woman" which is what I promised myself I would never do again.

The moral of this story is that we must make tough decisions. There is never clear guidance when it comes to making these decisions. Sometimes your gut will know what to do and sometimes you'll feel lost. I recommend making decisions that will better your future. Even if you have to pay a little extra in the end. I could have picked up a shitty job that would have covered my car insurance and registration but I truly believed that working for myself, no matter what happened, would work out for the best.

As I look back, I would have done the same thing all over again. I spent my money on food and things that would allow me to make more money down the road. I paid for gas to get to events to make new business relationships. I spent my money on courses that would teach me how to hold onto those relationships and how to sell products within them. I spent my money on equipment so I could raise my prices. When gigs only come in a couple of times a month, I could either go out and beg for more clients or just raise my prices. The quality of my work increased when I bought better equipment and clients didn't mind paying more when I handed them a better service or product. When I gave these clients a great product their peers wanted to hire me, and because I invested in myself I was able to build a larger list of clientele. In return, this makes me more money. Maybe not at first, but with time.

For example, I spent time and money on attending an event for barbers. I spent countless hours reaching out to barbers and tattoo artists and trying to acquire more customers, prior to the event. The only customers that I ended up with were interested in the same things I was; that would be motivating people and inspiring others to do the same. It's funny how it all works out. I stayed true to what I wanted and what I believed will benefit others in time. If I had picked up a couple of jobs to pay for my insurance and registration, yes, I would have been able to pay on time, but I would not have been able to attend the expo and meet higher paying customers. These customers have been paying me each month now and they are trying to make other people's lives better. If I got a job, I would have been miserable. I would have never been able to invest so much time and energy into this book or creating motivation products for you. It's simple in *my* mind.

Would I tell you not to pay your car insurance? No! Absolutely not. If you can pay it, pay it. It's a pain in the ass if you don't, as you can see. However, if you come to a very tough decision, follow your gut and it will always work out. I knew in my heart that investing in myself would get me further than paying for a "what if" I got into an accident. The probability that my car would get into an accident, while I was parked in my driveway, was really low. It was a risk worth taking to me. It's not just money you need to invest, it's time and energy as well. Make sure you have "Me" time and make sure you have "Me" money. This may sound backward to you, and everything you were taught, but this is my new way of thinking.

"If I invest in myself first, I will always be okay."

17

STILL NOT GETTING IT?

I f you're still not grasping the "pay yourself first" rule, let's try another avenue. Again, this is just used as an example and it's not guaranteed to work in your life. However, paying yourself first is an amazing principal that can be followed no matter what kind of life you lead. As I began telling you before, I purchased a digital camera that shot video and photos for about $600.00. I also talked about how I was charging my friends to take their headshots. Then, I started shooting video with the same camera. Actors also need reels, right? After auditioning for The American Academy of Dramatic Arts and having to prepare two monologues for it, I realized that other actors would need to do the same thing if they were applying for schools. Since I had been modeling before I went to school there, I had been seen at a few casting calls and had a couple of callbacks. In these callbacks, the producer and director would be on Skype viewing my audition in Boston, while enjoying the hot sun in Los Angeles.

I thought to myself, *That must happen so often.*

So what did I do? I started filming my friends acting out their monologues but shot it with my video camera in a setting that seemed to fit the script. Similar to what Matt Stannah needed. I didn't make a production out of it but it worked. The actors would send their monologue to casting agents, directors, producers, and who knows who else. I started charging for it. Each video was $100.00 and we took as many takes as we needed to until it was what they were trying to portray as the character.

One thing led to another and I had to learn how to edit these monologue videos to add the actor's name, number, email address, and/or agent's contact. Since I had to teach myself how to edit and color the footage so it looked like a scene from a movie, I was able to start charging for editing services as well. Next thing I know, I had a little movie production company that I had started alongside my photography company. Both of them were under the same umbrella at the time, as tHAt Entertainment. It got really confusing for clients when I kept learning new skills and adding them as services to my website, so I had to learn how to design websites and online portfolios too. Obviously, I invested more than $600.00 because as I started making my money back I would buy better equipment. Better lenses would enhance the quality. I bought a reflector to bounce light into my client's eyes for headshots.

I kept investing in myself and paying myself first, so I was able to buy more equipment that raised the bar for the quality of my work. It becomes a snowball effect, not long after committing to what you want to invest your money in. It's important to set goals that involve that money you are putting off to the side for investing or otherwise that money will not be making you money. If you are saving it, your balance practically stays the same. If you invest in something you know nothing about, that's gambling and you will lose almost every time. When you invest in yourself, you are betting on the one person that you can count on in life. YOU! That's it. If you put your own money up for something that you know in your heart will be successful because you won't stop until it is, then you win every time. You may not make a ridiculously huge return on your investment at first and you might not even see the ROI until years later. Then it dawns on you that you paid for the learning experience at the very least. You learned lessons and now you're able to make better decisions and have better judgment on the next go around.

Do a little math with me here. Initially, I was out of pocket $600.00, right? It started out rough. I was charging $50.00 per shoot. Let's do the math on the lowest rate I charged to see how many shoots I would need to do at that rate, in order to start making a profit. Divide $600.00 by $50.00 and I'd have to take on 12 shoots in order to make all of my investment money back. Obviously, as soon as shoot 13 rolled around I would have made a $50.00 profit. How cool is that? This just gets me excited writing about it. With all the time I had invested in each shoot and the editing, it would have taken me longer to make a profit but if we were going off of funds withdrawn from my bank account and income deposited into my bank account, that's the math.

"Great! Now we have a number to work with."

Realistically, at the time I was probably only able to take on 1 or 2 shoots per month because I was working 2 or 3 jobs in addition to this new entrepreneurial endeavor. Let's just say I was able to take on 1 shoot a month. It would take me 12 months, obviously, to make my money back. However, on that 13 month, I would have made $50.00.

Shall we compare our Return On Investment, or ROI, to the APY of your average savings account at a bank? You know, the one Mom, Dad, and everyone else told you open in order to get super rich? I'll compare traditional savings accounts from 2 well-known banks and the "Invest In Yourself" account I have been talking to you about. It's for you to decide which one you would like to put your money into after you see the math:

~

The first APY rate will be the rate from a very well known bank who I will not name but we will call them "Pursuit Bank." I will be using synonyms of their names so you can go see for yourself when you figure it out. Deal? The second one will be called "Observe Bank." The third account will be called "My Bank" which is, well, my bank account for investing in myself.

There are some terms and conditions for this experimental math problem we will be working on here. Before I get into it with you, I want to tell you what Annual Percentage Yield means. It will be replaced by the letters APY as you will soon see for yourself. An Annual Percentage Yield is just what it sounds like. After one year or twelves months, however you want to say it, of letting the bank use your money to make investments for themselves, they will give you a percentage of your money back, in addition to what you lent to them twelve months prior. The percentage that they will give back to you is called the APY. It's just a little fun fact for you and a reminder if you already knew that. It's also called interest. I don't like using this term because it's only in the interest of the bank. There are no benefits to you.

Let's get started! Firstly, Pursuit Bank has an Annual Percentage Yield, otherwise known as APY, of .03% for their savings account. Secondly, Observe Bank has an APY of 1.20% when you open a savings account with them, because they are an online banking service and they have very few locations that they need to pay for. For this reason, they have a higher APY than Pursuit Bank. Still with me? Awesome.

"Isaac, what happened to My Bank?"

Well, right now, all we know is that My Bank made no profit in 12 months and made $50.00 at the end of the 13th month, right? So we are about to calculate what we know, in order to compare all three. Below, I will walk you through this, step by step. Here's what we have so far:

PURSUIT BANK	OBSERVE BANK	MY BANK
APY = .03%	APY = 1.20%	APY = TBD%

Now, because I spent $600.00 and bought a camera kit that I was hoping made me a profit, I will also pretend to deposit $600.00 into the other two bank accounts. We need to start with an even score. Each account will begin with $600.00 in it. Would you agree that the balance in My Bank account would be equal to zero after I spent $600.00? Yes! Obviously. So either way, I am putting $600.00 somewhere that I cannot touch for a year. Whether it's a savings account or a camera. Here's what I will do, I will show you a month to month comparison for 12 months, 13 months, and what happens after 24 months as we move forward. First, I need to turn the percentages into decimals so we can figure this out correctly. This is taking us back to basic math but I told you I'd walk you through, step by step. To turn a percentage into a decimal we must divide by 100. If we have 10% and want to find out what the decimal is we need to divide 10 by 100. Our answer equals .10 as a decimal. See the tables below with both of our bank's APYs divided by 100 to figure out our decimals for each account.

PERCENT TO DECIMAL
10 ÷ 100 = .10

OBSERVE BANK APY	
APY 1.20%	1.20 ÷ 100 = 0.012
BANK'S APY AS A DECIMAL	
APY 1.20%	

PURSUIT BANK APY	
APY .03%	.03 ÷ 100 = 0.0003
BANK'S APY AS A DECIMAL	
APY 0.0003%	

Okay, this is where it starts getting a little ugly and a bit tricky. Luckily, I spent all day yesterday trying working out all the kinks for you. That makes today a lot easier for me and hopefully, you'll be able to understand it better. Ready?

Now that we have each bank's APY in decimal form, we are able to multiply it by the $600.00 we have put into the bank. The product will be what you made for profit after 12 months. See below.

PURSUIT BANK
$600 x 0.0003 = 0.18
TOTAL PROFIT PER YEAR
$0.18

I know! You're looking at that and saying, *"What the actual fuck is that? Did he even do the math correctly? I make 18 cents after 12 months?"*

Well, my friend, I hate to break it to you, but I most certainly did do that math correctly. I feel your pain which is why I would never use Pursuit Bank for a savings account ever again. I found Observe Bank after I saw that. They were a little better. Not much but clearly better. Check it out.

OBSERVE BANK
$600 x 0.012 = 7.20
TOTAL PROFIT PER YEAR
$7.20

Now you may look at this and say, *"Okay, that's dope. I would make a lot more with bank number two."*

You're correct, but you are still only making $7.20 after letting the bank use $600.00 of your hard earned money, for a whole year! That's absurd! I don't know about you, but that makes me want to take my money and never even give it to the bank. They're making trillions and trillions of dollars off of all the people that lend the bank their hard earned money and all they can give back in return is less than 2%? This is just the beginning.

Should we totally eliminate Pursuit Bank from this rest of this experiment? Okay! I'm glad you agree. It's not even worth calling them a fucking bank anymore. From here on we will only use Observe Bank and My Bank to demonstrate returns at the end of the thirteenth month period. I said earlier that I was going to give you a month to month look at this as well. The more info you have, the easier it will be for you to make better decisions when the time comes. When it comes to figuring out how much profit was made each month from a $600 "investment" at Observe Bank, we need to divide our profit of $7.20 by twelve months.

OBSERVE BANK
Profit Per Year = $7.20
THE MATH
Profit Per Year ÷ 12 Months = Profit Per Month
$7.20 ÷ 12 = $0.60
PROFIT PER MONTH
Profit Per Year = $0.60

From here, we take the Profit Per Month and watch our $600.00 grow across twelve months. The Profit Per Month is added to the balance at the end of each month. For example, January's ending balance would be $600.60.

OBSERVE BANK - MONTHLY BALANCE					
1	2	3	4	5	6
JAN	FEB	MAR	APR	MAY	JUNE
$600.60	$601.20	$601.60	$602.40	$603.00	$603.60
7	8	9	10	11	12
JUL	AUG	SEP	OCT	NOV	DEC
$604.20	$604.80	$605.40	$606.00	$606.60	$607.20

If we were to do the same thing for My Bank, we would have to do this a little differently. With a bank, you would see what you deposited at the start plus the Profit Per Month. When we look at My Bank, we have to start with a balance of $0.00 and add $50 per month to the balance as I make my money back by acquiring one shoot each month. That is ridiculously low but it's how I started out. Here we go.

MY BANK - MONTHLY BALANCE					
1	2	3	4	5	6
JAN	FEB	MAR	APR	MAY	JUNE
$50.00	$100.00	$150.00	$200.00	$250.00	$300.00
7	8	9	10	11	12
JUL	AUG	SEP	OCT	NOV	DEC
$350.00	$400.00	$450.00	$500.00	$550.00	$600.00

Alright, so I have made zero profit in twelve months as you can see in the My Bank account. The Observe Bank account has profited $7.20 in twelve months. Let's see what happens on the thirteenth month, shall we? Now I could just take $0.60 and add that to the balance at the end of January but that math would be wrong. Here's why. We now have a new balance of $607.20 in our Observe account if we don't touch our investment money. Let's leave the money in there and do all the math again for our new investment balance. After we multiply our new balance by our APY of .012, then we will divide that answer by twelve, so we can see what the proper number should be to add at the end of the of January.

OBSERVE BANK		
$607.20 x 0.012 = $7.2864		
$7.2864 ÷ 12 = $0.6072		

12		13
DEC		JAN
$607.20	+ $0.6072 =	$607.8072

When we hit the 13th month after accruing interest in our Observe Account, we end up with a whopping balance of $607.8072. Now let's look at My Bank account. Remember, we are adding $50.00 per month to this account since we opened it.

12		13
DEC		JAN
$600.00	+ $50.00 =	$650.00

MY BANK		
Profit ÷ New Balance = Decimal Interest Rate x 100 = Percentage Interest Rate		
$50 ÷ $600 = 0.0833 x 100% = 8.33%		

Our My Bank interest rate is 8.33% after we're successful with our math.

13 MONTH INTEREST RATE
8.33%

That's crazy, right? That's at least 6 times higher than Observe Bank. To be honest, I didn't realize how much of a difference this was until I started writing this book but I just knew I was making more money by investing in myself. Just so you know that I am beyond serious about this, I want to show you what the forecast would look like for you after 2 years, or 24 months, for both accounts, side by side. The interest rate changes over time for My Bank when I continuously keep depositing $50.00 each month. The difference is staggering!

	13 MONTHS	
	OBSERVE BANK	MY BANK
	$600 x 0.012 = $7.20	$50 x 13 = $650
	$600 + $7.20 = $607.20	
	$607.20 + $0.6072 (Month 13's Interest) = $607.8072	
NEW BALANCE	$607.8072	$650
PROFIT	$7.8072	$50
ROI %	1.30%	8.33%

	2 YEARs (24 MONTHS)	
	OBSERVE BANK	MY BANK
	$607.20 x 0.012 = $7.2864	$50 x 24 = $1,200
	$607.20 + $7.2864 = $614.4864	
NEW BALANCE	$614.4864	$1,200
PROFIT	$14.4864	$600
ROI %	2.41%	100%
DIFFERENCE	97.59%	

Yes! You read that correctly! I can't stress how important this is. That's 97.59% more return on your investment than the traditional way we were taught in high school. It's outrageous. Granted, there are some people that say that you should put your money on a CD or a 401K, etc. Yes, those will pay more than a savings account at Observe Bank but even then, you have absolutely zero control over your ROI! Why on earth would you give your money to someone else and trust that they have YOUR best interests in mind? That's just stupid. The highest rate that I just found when I looked was from one of the most well-known banks on the planet and their CD rates were 2.45% APY for 6 years. That means you have to give them your hard earned money for a minimum of 6 years, or you are charged a fee when you withdraw. The fee will end up being more than the profit you would make on a rate so small. It's ridiculous. If you can't tell, this drives me nuts. It should drive you nuts too. Let's do some math on a CD Rate from a bank we'll call Silver Women and Saxophone.

SILVER WOMAN AND SAXOPHONE BANK		RETURN ON INVESTMENT	NEW BALANCE
Deposit	$600.00		
Year 1	$600 x 0.0245 = $14.70	$14.70	$614.70
Year 2	$614.70 x 0.0245 = $15.06	$29.76	$629.76
Year 3	$629.76 x 0.0245 = $15.43	$45.19	$645.19
Year 4	$645.19 x 0.0245 = $15.81	$61.00	$661.00
Year 5	$661 x 0.0245 = $16.19	$77.19	$677.19
Year 6	$677.19 x 0.0245 = $16.59	$93.78	$693.78
6 YR ROI%	$93.78 ÷ $600 = 0,1563 x 100% =	**15.63%**	

As we do, I will compare this "better" interest rate to my plan of attack and see who wins. I know this is like beating a dead horse but the more you look at the numbers, the more likely it will trigger a good habit. This is something you need to see to believe.

I will multiply $50.00 times 72 months and see what we get. Then I will calculate what our return on investment is. Remember, this is assuming I make at least an average of $50.00 per month. After 6 years of being in business, I will have raised my prices so high that I would have to do all of this math all over again. This is basically as low as I can get unless I stopped shooting entirely. Even if you were to factor that in, it would still be worth investing in yourself. Again, who taught us this? If you came from a rich family, maybe you already knew this and this book wasn't meant for you. If you're like me and you were raised on the low end of the middle class or you were lower class and poor, then this will change your life, I promise!

	SWS BANK	MY BANK
Year 6	See Previous Table	$50 x 72 (Months) = $3,600
PROFIT	$93.78	$3,000
	$93.78 ÷ $600 = 0.1563 x 100% =	$3,000 ÷ $600 = 5 x 100% =
6 YR ROI%	15.63%	500%

You see the math. You see how much better it is to invest in yourself, first. It's hard to argue with this, in my opinion. As the great Chris Rock said in *Comedians In Cars Getting Coffee*,

"There's math and everything else is debatable."

18

WHY SHOULD I LISTEN TO YOU?

I know! It's insane! I am really trying to prove both sides here. It's hard to come at this without being bias towards my way of doing business and banking. In addition to that, I had a hard time coming up with these charts for you because I kept thinking, *Who the fuck wants to learn the language of money from someone who isn't at least a millionaire yet?*

Am I right? As Tai Lopez says, "What's their worth a damn factor?"

My advice is worth a damn because I have been able to create multiple businesses with this method. I won't list them all out here but just to name a few, Isaac Danna Photography, Stick With That Entertainment, Scratch That Music, Red Soil Productions, and I'm working on creating my biggest business to date that will be called Danna University. Plus, I'm happy as fuck when I wake up almost every morning. Can you say the same thing? If not, that's why I wrote this book. I hope it triggers something that makes you smile.

I invested in myself, which meant that I was able to buy new equipment and pay for courses, classes, and streams of conferences where multi-billion dollar business owners discuss what they have learned from trial and error. When you try to keep track of your ROI when it comes to investing in yourself, it becomes nearly impossible very quickly. The reason for that is that the amount of knowledge you are able to acquire from one talk or one lesson that costs you $250.00, could benefit your business model so much it becomes priceless. Yes, there are some shitty (I do mean shitty) courses out there that aren't worth the money but that's okay. Do you know why? It's okay because you are still learning even when the course sucks. It's okay because with the "Pay Yourself First" mindset you will make your money back so much faster than traditional methods, you'll be able to try another course whenever you want. The ROI really becomes priceless.

For me specifically, I ended up with a salary job that paid $50,000 per year. That's great. When I started putting money aside and *not* paying other people before myself, I was able to save $12,000 in 6 months. Let's talk a little bit about what I created my "investment" account for. I stopped calling it a savings account because I wasn't saving the money. Instead, I came up with a game plan. (Google Drive is an extremely beneficial piece of software. Using Google Drive allowed me to create a spreadsheet which you can see on the following pages.

When you look at it, I have it all laid out by bank account. This particular spreadsheet doesn't have interest rates because, at the time, I just started getting into this way of thinking. My skills weren't where they are now when it comes to designing spreadsheets and charts. However, this spreadsheet shows you that each month I was putting away quite a bit of money. Some months were better than others, but I had a goal of $24,000. That was *my* goal. It's actually the wrong thing to do though, as I didn't know I needed to specify what I wanted to do with the $24,000 when I reached my goal. That's the best way to do it. At the time, I was just trying to beat my calculations each week and I turned it into a game. You can see that on Wednesday, February 3rd, 2016 I had hit an all-time high of $11,854.92. I remember having another couple of hundred dollars (cash) stashed away in my apartment as well. That would make the balance over $12,000.00. After that, you see the balance drop significantly a week later. I ended up buying an LED lighting kit for over $3,000.

This would allow me to shoot in darker locations and it also allowed me to raise my price when I was able to say, "Yes, I have lights. Don't worry!"

The more equipment I could include, when it came to shooting photo or video, the more it made it look like the value of my product or service was a lot higher than what the client was paying me. Unfortunately, I don't have the months prior to November 2015 in this chart. I can't remember when I started reading *Rich Dad Poor Dad* but I know it was late in 2015, which means I started saving a little bit of money before that without reading. That makes me really happy.

A few other things I was able to buy with this investment money was a professional mirrorless camera for $3,200. One that some professionals didn't even have yet and that was on my list for a long time. I was able to travel to Wales for Christmas with my girlfriend at the time which was awesome because, for the first time in our relationship, I was actually taking care of myself. It was a wonderful feeling. I can't really explain it. Also, since the money was already aside for the trip it didn't feel like I had to rip my heart out when I paid for it.

Another thing I bought was my Ford Escape. The one that I got towed the other day. Twice. I was going through some shit with the lady and I was looking for a truck to sleep in if the breakup went badly. I found my baby for $2,500. After that, I ended breaking up with my girlfriend and she moved back to the United Kingdom. That left me with covering the entire rent for as long as I could and that ended up only being for about two months or so. The rent was $1,600. Two months later I spent a total of $3,200 of my hard earned money on a place to live. It was fucking ridiculous. That's the part of this I hated, that entire account was supposed to pay for equipment and learning. Not rent! Then I quit my job and started from square one ALL OVER AGAIN!

		Day Of Week	Date	Chase Checking	TD Saving	Paypal	Grand Total	Goal	To Hit Goal	Minimum Savings/Month	Months Left	Target Date	Estimated Date	Months Ahead of Schedule
2015		Monday	11/16/2015	$4,934.41	$1,330.90	$441.91	$6,707.22	$24,000.00	$17,292.78	1000	17.29	9/24/2017	4/25/2017	5 Months Ahead
		Tuesday	11/17/2015	$4,934.41	$1,630.90	$441.91	$7,007.22	$24,000.00	$16,992.78	1000	16.99	9/24/2017	4/17/2017	5 Months Ahead
	Nov	Wednesday	11/18/2015	$4,934.41	$1,884.52	$647.84	$7,466.77	$24,000.00	$16,533.23	1000	16.53	9/24/2017	4/3/2017	5.5 Months Ahead
		Monday	11/23/2015	$4,934.41	$2,211.86	$647.84	$7,794.11	$24,000.00	$16,205.89	1000	16.21	9/24/2017	4/3/2017	5.5 Months Ahead
		Wednesday	11/25/2015	$4,934.41	$2,465.50	$647.84	$8,047.75	$24,000.00	$15,952.25	1000	15.95	9/24/2017	3/24/2017	6 Months Ahead
		Tuesday	12/1/2015	$5,000.00	$2,709.98	$647.84	$8,357.82	$24,000.00	$15,642.18	1000	15.64	9/24/2017		
		Wednesday	12/2/2015	$5,000.00	$2,963.61	$647.84	$8,611.45	$24,000.00	$15,388.55	1000	15.39	9/24/2017		
	Dec	Monday	12/7/2015	$5,000.00	$2,963.61	$1,022.85	$8,986.46	$24,000.00	$15,013.54	1000	15.01	9/24/2017	3/7/2017	
		Wednesday	12/9/2015	$4,940.00	$3,417.24	$1,022.85	$9,380.09	$24,000.00	$14,619.91	1000	14.62	9/24/2017	3/7/2017	
		Monday	12/14/2015	$4,940.00	$3,417.24	$987.68	$9,344.92	$24,000.00	$14,655.08	1000	14.66	9/24/2017	3/7/2017	
		Wednesday	12/16/2015	$0.00	$9,798.54	$0.00	$9,798.54	$24,000.00	$14,201.46	1000	14.20	9/24/2017	3/7/2017	
		Thursday	12/31/2015	$0.00	$10,306.09	$0.00	$10,306.09	$24,000.00	$13,693.91	1000	13.69	9/24/2017	3/7/2017	
2016		Monday	1/4/2016	$0.00	$10,306.09	$0.00	$10,306.09	$24,000.00	$13,693.91	1000	13.69	9/24/2017	3/7/2017	
		Thursday	1/7/2016	$0.00	$10,560.16	$0.00	$10,560.16	$24,000.00	$13,439.84	1000	13.44	9/24/2017	2/21/2017	
	Jan	Wednesday	1/13/2016	$0.00	$11,014.24	$0.00	$11,014.24	$24,000.00	$12,985.76	1000	12.99	9/24/2017	2/13/2017	
		Wednesday	1/20/2016	$0.00	$11,268.30	$0.00	$11,268.30	$24,000.00	$12,731.70	1000	12.73	9/24/2017	2/13/2017	
		Tuesday	1/26/2016	$0.00	$11,338.30	$0.00	$11,338.30	$24,000.00	$12,661.70	1000	12.66	9/24/2017	2/13/2017	
		Wednesday	1/27/2016	$0.00	$11,592.38	$0.00	$11,592.38	$24,000.00	$12,407.62	1000	12.41	9/24/2017	2/13/2017	
		Wednesday	2/3/2016	$0.00	$11,854.92	$0.00	$11,854.92	$24,000.00	$12,145.08	1000	12.15	9/24/2017	2/13/2017	
	Feb	Wednesday	2/10/2016	$0.00	$8,374.90	$0.00	$8,374.90	$24,000.00	$15,625.10	1000	15.63	9/24/2017	2/13/2017	
		Thursday	2/11/2016	$0.00	$8,700.90	$0.00	$8,700.90	$24,000.00	$15,299.10	1000	15.30	9/24/2017	2/13/2017	
		Saturday	2/20/2016	$0.00	$2,142.99	$0.00	$2,142.99	$24,000.00	$21,857.01	100	218.57	9/24/2017		

19

THE TIPPING POINT

I t was at this point that I ran out of money. I was living in an apartment that I couldn't afford by myself after I broke up with my girlfriend that I was no longer in love with, and to top it off I was working at a job I hated. I had been working there for almost a year when I decided, enough was enough. I totally flipped my life around. Feeling depressed and lost as soon as I woke up every morning was not something to look forward to each day. I had to make a change or I wouldn't have wanted to wake up again. I never would have actually committed suicide because I knew life was too beautiful to give up but the thoughts of never waking up again definitely crossed my mind.

Wouldn't it be easier to not wake up tomorrow? All of this bullshit would just go away.

That's what would pass through my mind every night before bed. I cried myself to sleep on several occasions even back when I had my girlfriend to hold me and tell me everything was going to be okay.

I remember feeling like, *She's just saying that to try and make me feel better but she has no way of knowing for sure.*

It was rough.

Before I broke up with her, I had "everything" you're supposed to have to be happy. I was saving $1,000 each month, I was able to pay all my bills on time, I had a beautiful, loving girlfriend, her parents were incredible, I had a $50,000 salary job with two weeks vacation, I could walk to work because it was so close, I was living in an apartment in an up and coming part of Brooklyn, and it still seemed like I wasn't able to hit my full potential. Something was missing. She was in love with me and probably would have said, "yes," if I asked her to marry me. I had enough money saved to buy her a beautiful ring, instead of camera equipment or courses. My life was on the same path everyone else's was on. It seems like a good life right? WRONG! From the outside looking in, people saw me as successful. People said I was doing well for myself. On the inside, I struggled to smile. You would never know it by looking at my Facebook or Instagram. You would think with all the traveling and "fun" photos, that I would be living a very good life. I actually had a few people tell me, "I'm so jealous!"

Jealous of what?

I was no longer in love with my girlfriend. I hate to say this but it seemed like we were making better roommates than lovers. It wasn't a week of this feeling, it was months that turned into years of the same feeling. I don't want to be disrespectful, so I will leave that where it is because I still love her as a person who changed my life and for that, I am beyond thankful. She took care of me for years. Literally, paying my rent, buying groceries and flights when we traveled. I felt like I owed her everything. I felt like I wasn't good enough to be with someone that treated me so well. It became degrading. I felt like I was unable to provide for her and wasn't providing for her, for years. Until I landed the job that paid 50K a year, but that was the next problem. I knew that I wanted to save money and pay her back for what she did for me. I took that job because it didn't feel right not to when the opportunity arose. For the first time, I was going to be able to take her out and spoil her a little bit. Instead, I saved it all and ended the relationship. I kept coming home and saying, "I am not happy!"

She kept telling me, "It's the job. It's the job. Maybe it's seasonal depression."

No! It was the fact that I was no longer in love with her and it was suffocating when I felt like I was faking it. On top of that, I was going to work every day and doing stupid, pointless shit, that was never going to help anyone but the drunkards that were regulars at these bars I was managing. I wasn't pushing myself at all. The job was ridiculously easy, but I wanted to be the owner of the company. Once again, I wanted to be on the inside of those closed doors and see what happened at the top of the food chain.

I had my own indie production companies now and I was making a little money here and there on the weekends. Sometimes after my full-time job and my second job, I would set up a paid shoot or shoot for dirt cheap just to remind myself that I wanted to produce videos and take photos. It was not enough of an income to turn my dream into a full-time gig though, which is what needed to happen. Have you ever felt like you were meant for more? Have you ever felt like people don't understand you?

Have you ever felt lost and out of place? Almost as if you were non-existent? Especially when you can't relate to how boring traditional lifestyles are? I couldn't wrap my head around why all my friends and family thought I was doing so well.

Then it happened, I had one phone call with my father when I was at work. He asked how my girlfriend was doing. At this time, I was twenty-five and about to cry to him on the phone. (Wouldn't be the first time. What else do you do when your life isn't where you thought it would be? Crying is a great start in my opinion. It helps, trust me. Sometimes I allow myself to fully work through my emotions and it's such a relief.)

Anyways, I was on the phone and he said, "How're things? How's your girlfriend?"

I said, "Good. Same old, same old."

"Isaac! It's been 'Good. Same old, same old,' for years now. What are you going to do about it?"

That hit me hard enough to remember it and tell you. That's when I knew that I had to do whatever it took to make a change in my life. There was no right or wrong way to go about this, it was time. I had to get over the fact that I was about to hurt someone else's feelings and start looking after myself and what I wanted in life. It's not as easy as it sounds. I started to come up with a game plan on where I could move to. I'd give her the apartment since it was my decision to end things. I was going to buy a car and whatever I had left was going to be for equipment. The investment fund was going to be used differently than I wanted but for the first time in my entire life, I was fully capable of being able to afford my own place if I remained at the job that I hated.

Doesn't that sound worth it?

I had to do what I had to do. I would just work my ass off again to create a "pay yourself first fund" if it came to that. We eventually did break up and she ended up moving back home, as I said. That's why I was able to use a lot of the money on equipment because I didn't need first, last, and security for a new place. That was a pro.

I was happy for all of about two days before I had to go back to work in order to make money. I hated the job so much. At first, it was amazing. I got to run a small crew and build a bar from the ground up, which was great. Then, the funding from the investors for the next project was nowhere to be found and I was stuck painting chalkboards and replacing beautiful old hardwood floors with shitty plywood. The quality of my work was decreasing and my skills were not being used. I was actually forgetting how to do certain things that were fairly common to remember when working with wood. Little secret techniques were disappearing because I wasn't around highly skilled woodworkers or intelligent craftsmen. My bosses wanted to control the creative side of everything and then just have me build their design. That's not how I operate. Even if their design was actually pretty cool, I would struggle to create it because the tools in the shop were not meant for such intricate projects. Everything I touched felt like I half-assed it. I stopped giving a flying fuck while I was working. In fact, I was working on my own shit while I was working there. All day, I'd be watching Youtube videos on how to perfect my video editing or photoshop skills, how to create money online, or searching for places to print my photobooks.

. . .

That's something I totally forgot to tell you. There are just too many things I want to discuss with you.

I knew there was something else I spent my money on.

There was a company that I had used to print a coffee table book filled with three hundred and sixty-five pages of #isaacdannadaily. That was when I challenged myself to post a photo a day for a year. I am very proud to say that you can find my successful project on Instagram when you search for the hashtag. (Side note, please do not use the hashtag because that will ruin the complete set.) That book motivated me to create a smaller book, find printers, materials, ISBN barcodes, and all kinds of shit. That was my first physical product; I had designed a coffee table booklet. There are over twenty-five pages of artistically organized New York City photography in it, and it's all my work. I spent just over $1,000 to print one thousand copies. The plan was to walk around Times Square and sell them.

If the book cost me just over a dollar to print and I could sell it for five dollars, *We were in the money, baby!*

In theory.

So I spent the money on those books and one day I was sitting at work, the books had just arrived, and I thought, *Fuck this! I'm so done with this place. I'm going to walk around and sell these and make more money doing that than I would be working here.*

"Ey, boss! Can I talk to you," after invading his office space.

"Sure. What's up, buddy?"

Fired up and determined, "I can't work here anymore."

He was so upset. I could see it in his eyes. It was so hard. I felt like everyone around me would look at me as an idiot for leaving such a cushy job but it felt so right. I can't even explain how my stomach felt at this moment. The most relatable feeling is when I got on that school bus back in the day and had those butterflies on my first day of public school.

"In two weeks?" He asked.

I said, "No! Today...Sorry."

Mind you, this was first thing in the morning. I still had an entire day to work.

"Can I at least have a week, Isaac? Please?"

I didn't know what else to say because I felt bad, so I agreed. One week from that moment I'd be a free man. I was going to be a billionaire off of selling photo books in Times Square and anything else I wanted to try and pursue. All day, like every other day of work, I was on the computer and my emotions were building. I was getting more and more furious throughout the day. I felt like I didn't get what I wanted. I wanted to leave that day, cold turkey as they did in the movies. A middle finger and a smile from ear to ear.

Right before I was about to leave for the day, I grew a pair of balls and walked into his office again, "Ey, Boss?"

"What, Isaac? Don't do this to me!" He said.

He actually sounded sad, sadder than I was, and at that moment I was balling my eyes out because I had just lost control of my emotions completely. It wasn't quite the cinematic experience I was going for.

"Listen, I hate to do this to you but you have to understand, I'm an entrepreneur."

"...me too, Isaac."

"I know, I know. So can you understand that I want to leave so I can come back one day and actually own a bar with you? I want to be partners at some point and not an employee."

He respected that, as much as he could, "I get it, Isaac. I respect that but now I have to find someone else and I can't get them in here by tomorrow."

I said, "Here's what I'll do, alright? Listen, I only live right down the street. As soon as you find someone that you think is a good fit, I will come back and personally train them for free. No pay. I don't care. I just can't work here anymore. I don't want to fuck you over but I've literally been at my desk all day watching Youtube videos that will help me and my business, not yours. You are wasting money by keeping me on board. Time and money."

Being a businessman himself, he knew the value of time and money.

"Okay," releasing a sigh, "Good Luck," he said to me as he spun his chair around after giving me a goodbye handshake.

That meant the world to me. He was pissed but kept his composure and I could tell that he saw a little piece of him standing in front of him. He had no choice but to let me go. In all honesty, I hope I make enough money to go back and partner with him; to buy a couple of bars just for fun. Legit. I walked down to the shop and grabbed my tools, still balling my eyes out, and was about to walk to my second, part-time job, and finish up the evening there. That's when the feeling came over me again.

I hate this shit! I'm done!

I called my second boss and told him I will no longer be coming in. His shop was just one block away from where I was standing but I didn't want to experience what I just went through, again. Face-to-face was horrible. I think it's very important to have these face-to-face conversations because it builds character, and I am not just saying that. It toughens you up a bit.

"What the fuck, Bro? Are you serious? Isaac!" He said.

"Sorry, man. I know."

"No! Dude, I need you to finish this job. You can't just quit in the middle of it!" He said.

I wanted to say, *"Watch me,"* but I didn't.

He said, "I will pay you $1,000 each day this weekend to help me finish this job."

I said without even thinking about it, "It's not about the money, man."

"Oh, it's about the money, man," he yelled back into the phone.

I said, "No! It's not. I am so over this line of work." This conversation was actually easier than the last one because it was more aggressive and I was angry with life and work, all at the same time, so it felt right.

"Here's what I'll do. For you, I will finish sanding the table tops this evening. Then I'm done, okay?" I said.

"Okay." Then he hung up.

This was Chris, the boss that I really got along with, too. He was close to my age and shit, so we had fun working together but not enough to *not* make this awkward. When I showed up at the shop, he wasn't there. If I could show you how fucking fast I sanded those table tops, you would think I had mental problems. I wanted to sand them before he got back but obviously, that wouldn't happen. This was meant to happen face to face.

He came in and just laughed at me. Literally, laughed at me as if my dreams and goals didn't matter what so ever. I watched a "friend" disappear in front of my eyes. I saw it fade. We were only friends because he needed a hand and I was his "right-hand man." Unfortunately, it took me a really long time to realize that.

As I look back, I think about him telling me, "Oh, it's about the money, man!"

Is it? Is it about the money? Is it about working at a job you can't wait to leave? Is about taking jobs that you know you have no desire to take, just because it pays well? What does "It pays well" even mean? Is that money worth it when you have to skip holiday dinners with your family? Is it worth it when you're called into work during a blizzard and the governor has declared a state of emergency? Is it worth all the stressful evenings lying next to your significant other, pissed off because work is on your mind, while you should be there, fully present, in the moment with that person?

No amount of money could replace the feeling of taking one of my parent's out to breakfast at 10:37 am, on a Tuesday morning, smack dab in the middle of the summer, nowhere near a holiday. Nothing can replace playing *Call of Duty* with my younger brother at 1 am on a Monday morning, because I know I can sleep in and reset if I need to. Nothing can replace the feeling of making your very first sale of a product you designed, created, and produced from just one idea that came to you right after a nap on a Thursday afternoon as you looked out over the parking lot of your apartment complex to see only your car parked there, while everyone else is staring at the clock waiting to punch out.

There are so many moments like this that some people will

never feel. I don't want you to be one of those people. I want you to work less, make more money, and love what you do day in and day out, even if it feels like you are going against everything you have been taught in the past. It's scary. It's exciting. It's the only way I know how to live, now.

20

THE BEST AND THE WORST FEELING IN THE WORLD

After making sure that the table tops were sanded to perfection and saying my goodbyes, I grabbed whatever tools I had laying around at Chris' shop and threw them in my backpack. As I walked out the door and hopped on my bike, there was a weight lifted off my shoulders. If the gravity pulling all the tools in my backpack wasn't holding me down, I would have floated straight up through the clouds and landed on the moon with a smile and tears flowing from my eyes, simultaneously. One day, I hope you experience this feeling. Leaving the job you hate is the most exhilarating experience. It's weird because there's a parallel feeling, right next to the feeling of freedom, that will make you want to walk back in and beg for your job back. It's how we're trained.

Everything I had learned, up until I was able to make my own decisions with a clear mind, had been corrupted by traditions passed down from previous generations. I was going against every single thing I was force fed to believe about the proper way of living a life and chasing the "American Dream." What is the "American Dream?" How can someone else tell you how to live your life? You only have one. How can the opinions of others be so engraved in your mind that you actually start to think that if you were to act upon your own thoughts, you would be breaking "the rules?" What rules? Who put these rules in place? Are they even rules or are they a way of life that everyone accepts as the only way just because they have given up on their own dreams?

I believe that people lose track of what they want and simply accept their current circumstances as fate. They think, "Well, this is where I am supposed to be at this time in my life." In some cases that's a great way to see things. In others, not so much.

For instance, I am currently writing this book from the basement of my Brother's Girlfriend's Mother's house. Do I want to be here right now? Absolutely not. Do I have to accept the fact that I am here because of all the decisions I had to make up until this point in my life? Yes! Without a doubt, I am where I am because I chose to be here. Will I accept this as my fate and complain about it every day for the rest of my life as I sit on a couch and wish for things to change? No! Understanding that I am where I am because I have chosen to be here makes me want to make better decisions. However, being here was one of my decisions I had to make as an entrepreneur trying to build an empire. According to the man who has a full-time job, a wife, kids, a big house, a fancy car, a dog and nice clothes, I would appear to "Not have my shit together."

It's even been said to me recently, "You're not living at home? Are you?"

In fact, I have "my shit together" so much that I know this

living situation is temporary and it needed to happen this way in order for me to write this book for you and for myself. It needed to happen this way in order for me to build digital courses as online products and begin designing the blueprint for Danna University.

"#plug"

Do you really think the other guy has his "shit together" more than I do? On the outside, yes, it may appear that way. Traditionally speaking, that would appear to be the case. In reality, the man looking down on me right now hates his job, is bored of his wife, loves his kids but never sees them, and hates that he can't wear a tee shirt to work even just once a week. Anger fills his heart when he can't afford to pay his mortgage each month and he has to pick up the dog shit because nobody else in the family knows how. I can relate with the dog shit comment because the same thing happens here at this residence. I am living and breathing in an environment where "This Man" is someone's idol. Why would that be anyone's idol at all? Ever? I'll tell you why.

Since I was old enough to work (illegally) I was taught that money was needed in order to pay the bills and live your life. Money was hard to come by and it was gone before you knew what to do with it.

"How do you make money?"

Well, maybe you can relate here, but I was taught that I had to work to earn a paycheck. I would exchange my time for money and the more time I exchanged for money, the more money I would make at the end of the next week. The most logical thing to do with this kind of information is to go out and grab as many jobs as you can and work as much as you can. You end up working so much that you only see your family in the evenings and occasionally, the weekend. What do you do in your free time? You look around and see what everyone else around you is doing with their free time and follow suit, right? Am I wrong?

"Well, Jonny is taking Karen and the boys to dinner one night a week and they head down The Cape once a year for vacation. That's what I will do."

Fair enough. The Cape sounds like it could be fun and who doesn't like someone else cooking for them and being served a nice hot meal? Jonny also has to go back to work on Monday and hates his job. Karen also hates her job and doesn't want to leave the kids with a babysitter or drop them off at daycare because she would rather spend time with them. It becomes a very stressful situation between the husband and wife and they don't feel like they can change their way of life. They spend whatever they have left after the bills (if they can even pay the bills) and they blow it on material things that are supposed to reward them with happiness.

Does this sound familiar? We're taught that work equals money and money equals happiness, but when you don't have the time to spend the money on meaningful things, the money ends up getting spent of material items that reward you with a quick burst of happiness. Maybe it's a beer to calm the nerves after work. Maybe it's a boat to explore the middle of the lake away from everyone else. Maybe it's a treehouse for the kids, so they can play outside, and you can spend time with your significant other inside. When it boils down to it, we are taught that going to college will make us more likable for obtaining a position at a corporate establishment. You'll be paying student loans for the rest of your life but that's okay, at least you get the chance to sit in a fucking cubical every day and use your paycheck to drink beer after your ten hour work day just to waste time with co-workers that you are forced to try and get along with.

What happens when you have an excessive amount of student loans and you are unhappy with the job you got. In fact, you're unhappy with life in general. The whole career choice is off. Then what? You start to think, "Fuck! I hate my life. I want to change it. What do I do? I'm stuck here because I spent so much money on school. I can't just get a new job. That would be a waste of money."

Why? Why can't you switch careers? You most certainly can. It's a mindset. Instead, people decide they want to go back to school just for the same thing to happen all over again. Why? It's a never-ending game. This time around you are actually more in debt and further and further from being current on your bills. You don't think this causes stress? Of course, it does, and you have every reason to be stressed in that position.

Here's the thing, it's not just you. It's everyone around you too. Who do you talk to about this when you're stressed? If you try and have this conversation with anyone around you they'll just spit out their sad story and try to "one-up" you. Everyone has fucking issues. It's important to remember that. It's also important to remember that if you feel bad or sorry for yourself you will end up very depressed. You will end up feeling helpless and stuck. In reality, you are. You're helpless and stuck. You know why? Because this is the outcome of all the decisions that you have made up until this point in your life. If you want a change, make a change. I will tell you right now, that nobody else actually gives a flying fuck about your issues because they have some too. They're too busy worrying about their own shit and gossiping about their neighbor's problems to make themselves feel better.

I know you know what I'm talking about. If you are in this position, I suggest that you take a step back and view your situation as a mechanic viewing a car. They'll try and find the problem. Why isn't the car running smoothly? What's the hissing noise? What's the rattling? They find the issue and fix it. The payment comes out of your pocket but you are paying to fix problems. Look at your life as a mechanic would look at your car. Where are the problems? What things are causing significant amounts of stress and why? How do you fix it? Take it one problem at a time but just start fixing it. If that means you need to leave the job you hate, do it. If it means you need to cut certain friends out of your life or maybe even toxic family members, do it. If you can't pay your bills, find a way to make more money. Remember what I said, work less and make more. Figure it out.

I am biased when it comes to creating entrepreneurs. I think working for yourself and answering to no one, ever, is the ultimate goal. That's my American Dream. Freedom! The only difference is, I am working towards my version of the American Dream every day. As someone who works for themselves, I can determine how long my lunch is. I decide whether or not I want to leave later, after dinner with my parents. I can decide whether or not I want to take on a job that my gut tells me not to take. I design my own schedule. Nobody is giving me orders when I am collaborating with other companies and clients. Yes, of course, we have moments where it may feel like you're working for someone else's vision but in the end, you can choose whether or not you want to work with that person again.

Don't get me wrong, on occasion, I will roll over in my bed and not want to do a damn thing, except to call up my old employers and cry, asking to sweep for a living. Do I actually do that? No. Will there be some days where I lack the motivation to get out of my bed? Yes, of course. Even then, who is making me go downstairs to the basement and work? Nobody. I have to make the decision to get out of those warm blankets and step on a cold floor if I want to keep designing the lifestyle I want to live. The added benefit is I can give myself a raise at any time and I can't fire myself. Therefore, if my output is low there is nobody else to blame but myself. Firing myself would result in having to pick up a 9-5 and I'm definitely *never* going back to that shit. That thought gets me out of bed pretty quick.

It's easier than you think but it's not for everyone. Some people like stability and I have been in business for over five years and there is no such thing for me, yet. Every morning, for a brief moment, I wonder where my next check is coming from. There are months that I can't afford my bills or the fees for not paying them. My credit score has dropped significantly, but it heading back up. This is all temporary and I truly believe that. I am not worried, at all. I know that by working on this book, it will help others get to where I am today. HAPPY AS FUCK. I wake up every morning, happy. HAPPY! No joke. Whether I know where the money is coming from or not, I am still happy. I know that making my motivational masterclass, *Wake Up Masterclass,* will help people find out who they truly are. I know that creating Danna University will help kids unleash their creative side while playing with software that will allow them to work from home or anywhere on planet earth for that matter.

Seriously, this is so much bigger than you and I. Once you realize that you can actually make a difference, even if it's for a small crowd of people, you will start to see things differently. I don't advise you to drop your job and ghost on them tomorrow, but I do want to tell you that it's an option. You can if you want to. I will say that you need to have some sort of grand scheme in order to make it work, though. If you don't and you just quit to be lazy, hardly working or working without a purpose, you'll end up more stressed and depressed than ever before. I don't mean that you have to work all the time. I will be the first to tell you that I enjoy video games and watching Netflix. (We still need chill time.) Just don't leave your job until you have a plan. A solid plan. I left my former career as a woodworker because I lost the love for it and I had a little bit of a game plan. Do I wish I stayed a little longer? Sometimes. Sometimes I wish I was making a lot more money too, but then I realize it's about helping other people and that the money will follow when I have stayed true to what I believe. You can start your own business venture if you want. You can work your way up the ladder at a job you already have. Just don't be blind to your situation, that's all I ask. I showed you the math when it comes to investing in yourself. Try it out.

When I look back, here's what I wish someone told me in school: Creating your own company is literally as easy as handing money over for a piece of paper. You don't need investors, you don't need a logo, you don't need partners, you don't even need experience. You can do it all on your own by saving a little bit of money and forming an LLC. That's it. You also don't need the binders that they sell you after you pay for the paperwork. You are paying for a piece of paper. How's this for logic, ready? This just came to me as I was writing this:

You can either save your money and pay for college or save your money and start a business that could become a college.

Either way, you are paying for a piece of paper or a certificate. That's it. A piece of paper will determine whether or not you have a degree or your very own business. It all comes down to paper being exchanged for paper. Graduating college will give you a piece of paper that will allow you to work for someone else that has a different piece of paper. The only difference is the cost of that piece of paper. You can acquire both if you really want too but to start your own business, it will cost less than student loans cost. You'll be paying for business classes on how to run a business or how to form a business and you can find all of that at the library, for free! If you don't want to use the library, use the library of the world wide web. You can start a business right from your bed, right now, or you can start a business from your desk at the job you despise. That's the ultimate slap in the face to your employer. It's not fucking hard. I hope I'm getting this across. Don't overthink it. Just do it. You don't need the big buildings, the warehouses, the trucks, the employees, the investors, the logos, the big ass signs, or lawyers. I couldn't make this shit up. All you need is an idea and a couple of hundred dollars. Seriously. Especially if you just want to create online businesses. Oh my God! That's even easier.

It all starts with what you want your life to look like. Be honest with yourself and I truly believe that will take you places. It will take you all over. Experiment and take your time. You may try forty-five thousand things you never want to do again, but when you find that one thing that ignites a little fire inside you, you'll know what path to follow. This got really inspirational and that was not what I intended, but I love the way this came out so I shall keep it and end with this:

I started raking leaves and mowing my grandfather's lawn. I moved onto the fryolator at a fast food, seafood company and then I moved up to the grill. From there I learned how to laminate countertops and build cabinets. After that, I learned how to operate a CNC machine. At nineteen, I worked my way up and began traveling the United States as a foreman on the trade show floor. I was in charge of six to tens guys that were at least thirty years older than I was. I followed my gut and moved to New York City to become an actor. I ended up becoming a filmmaking, male stripper trainee, shoe selling, clothes salesman, set builder for a theatre company. I ended up co-founding Red Soil Productions, Scratch That Music, and now I am the owner of Stick With That Entertainment. I've designed websites, logos, furniture, jewelry boxes, and clothing. After publishing this book, I will officially become an author. I host *That Podcast With Isaac Danna*. There are no rules or limits to what you can try and accomplish. Some things work out and others don't, but the one thing that continuously keeps working out for me is following my heart, instincts, gut or whatever you want to call it. It never fails me.

21

BUILD YOUR OWN EMPIRE

Not every business will cost you an idea and a few hundred dollars, but here are a few with extremely low start-up costs. If you have the drive to experiment to find which avenue you are most passionate about, the sky's the limit. Obviously, for anything online related you should have a computer. I will do my best to calculate for you what the start-up costs are estimated to be late 2017 - early 2018. Please adjust and redo the math if you are reading this in 2040. Don't ask why I picked that year, I just thought twenty, doubled, would be a cool year. Also, I want to point out that these are things that I am currently doing to make money. I wouldn't give you a list of things that I have not tried or enjoyed doing for myself. If I didn't know how successful these could be, I wouldn't recommend them to you.

Another side note before we begin, once you take care of the largest expenses (such as a computer, software, and fees for creating the company) you can literally just expand your business by simply offering another service for your customers. The tools for each of these are usually very similar and they don't vary much. Sometimes you need an extra plug-in or software upgrade that will cost you but the startup costs are less and less because you'll already own all the shit needed.

Smell what I'm steppin' in? Good! LET'S GO!

- **Photo-retouching Services** (Editorial, Headshots, Weddings, etc.)

- **Graphic Design Work** (Logos, Flyers, IG and FB ads, etc.)

- **HTML5 Website Design** (Portfolios, E-commerce, Blogs, etc.)

- **Video Editor** (Vlogs, Web Series, IG & FB Ads / Commercials, etc.)

- **Audio Mixer / Engineer** (Musician's Albums, Singles, Podcasts, etc.)

- **Music Production** (Instrumentals, Custom Scores, etc.)

- **Social Media Content Management** (Creating, Editing, Posting, Tracking, etc.)

These are the 7 that I can honestly recommend because I have made money with each of them or have been asked to do it for someone and turned it down. They're in high demand.. Let's go over the tools you will need in order to start freelancing or creating a business that includes these services. Remember, you don't need all the tools at once. You need to ease into learning each one and expand your business as your mind expands.

YOU WILL NEED

A laptop or a desktop
COST = $2,000+

If you do not have a computer already (which you should) you can buy refurbished or previously owned. Check eBay or Craigslist for used ones. I swear I just found a MacBook Pro 2013 with all the bells and whistles for under $500.00, including shipping, on eBay. You have to look and wait. Patience.

If you are buying new, I would highly recommend using B&H Photo and Video Store or Apple themselves. I have no idea about PCs, nor do I care, because I hate them. Deal with it. I've tried to go back to a PC and it's horrible when you try and switch back. I love everything about Apple computers.

You should have Adobe Creative Cloud
COST = $54/month

I highly, highly recommend the entire Cloud. Again, I HIGHLY recommend investing in yourself for this one. It's not worth the pain and trouble of finding a free version and having it crash in the middle of working for a paying customer. It's scary, trust me. This will run you about $54/month. I know, it seems like a lot but you'll make that money and a whole lot more very soon. Adobe Creative Cloud is the one thing I use every single day. The sky's the limit with all the apps that are included.

I use *Lightroom* for organizing my photos with its "Library" feature and sometimes I use it for editing RAW images from my camera, but I prefer DXO Optics Pro (10 and Up); this is not necessary, however. I think it's better in some areas so I use it in those areas but I could use Lightroom in its entirety if I wasn't a bit of a snob here.

I use *Photoshop* for fucking EVERYTHING! Legit. I use it to create ideas and inspire myself. I use it to eliminate whatever I no longer want in the image. I use it to color pick from images and create branded palettes for my clients as well as my own businesses. I've used it to make GIFs for ads and website content. I use it to retouch every single portrait I publish, no exceptions. I use it to design business cards, Facebook and Instagram content which could be doubled as an ad. I use it to edit product photos and place them on white backgrounds for e-commerce websites or ads. I use it in conjunction with *Illustrator* to create logos for clients or tweak existing logos. I use it to compress images so they load faster on websites. I create movie posters for IMDB and Youtube/Vimeo thumbnails. I use Photoshop so much, I can't even tell you all the things I use it for.

I use *Premiere Pro* for all of my video editing needs. It's handy when I need to create IG, Snapchat, or Facebook stories. You can create all kinds of sequence settings to adapt to each platform and save the preset so you are able to drag and drop footage into the timeline, chop that shit up, and publish it.

I use *Audition* to edit and mix audio that I seamlessly transfer from my Premiere Pro projects, and I can directly link the audio and markers in both softwares. This may sound like gibberish at the moment but I swear it's so helpful. I'll play with Logic in the near future.

I use *Illustrator* for all my logo needs. It's great for creating graphics that you can scale without losing any quality while increasing the size. I use it when I trace drawings and convert hand drawn text or logos into digital designs. It's epic. I told you, **The Sky's The Limit!**

The reason I suggest you have all these tools are because you never know what the client will want to adjust and add for content. Clients can be very lazy and they will want everything done for them. The more you know how to do, the better. If you can say that you know how to do something that they don't, you can charge a higher rate for that task. It may only take you another twenty minutes to perform the requested task in a second software but you can create an additional fee for that action and charge for an hour. Now you have forty minutes of free time, and they will recommend you and become a returning customer which is your bread and butter.

You NEED an Internet connection.
COST = FREE
(Free at a coffee shop, library or Friend's house)
Or you pay $50+ / month

I know this will sound quite ridiculous but I use the internet every single day and you should be using it as well. Not for Facebook and Instagram, but to learn. Watch tutorial videos on Youtube. Read blogs related to what you're trying to learn. Watch TED Talks and get inspired. Open your mind by downloading some E-Books or Audiobooks. I use it to access a number of different cloud apps and organize my documents, photos, and videos so it's one click away from my clients. I also use it to send invoices and quotes. I don't think I need to go into detail about how important the internet is to us. If you don't understand it yet, maybe you should just put this book down and see for yourself.

You need a Dropbox account.
COST = FREE
(Up to 2 GBs of Storage Space)

Then $10+/Month
(After you need to upgrade to 1TB)

I survived on the 2GBs for a long time because I kept asking my friends and family to download Dropbox on their computers when I would shoot for them. At the time, they would give you 500mbs of storage space for every one person you got to sign up and download it to a computer. I use it to share files with clients, to store some very important files I would like duplicates of (such as logos or something I need to access from anywhere), I even use it to receive files from clients or help them organize shit on their end. It's also another alternative to transfer your social media content from your computer to your phone. It works like a charm because most apps can import photos or images straight from Dropbox. I've noticed the integration more and more lately.

An alternative to Dropbox would be Google Drive.
However, I recommend you have both.
COST = FREE
(Up to 15 GBs of Storage Space)
Then $1.99+/month
(For up to 100 GBs or $10+/month for 1TB)

It's very similar to Dropbox. Each has its own benefits which are why I suggest learning both, even if you prefer one over the other. I started using Google Drive just before I started working at the $50,000/yr job. They were using it for their entire corporation. It became apparent to me that it was a software that just made sense. I am all about using common sense and trying to make my life as easy as possible so I can spend more time NOT working. The bonus of using Google Drive is that you can download or upload files like you would any other software but you have Google Sheets as well which is really helpful for creating spreadsheets and business plans. I haven't found that sort of thing using Dropbox, but maybe I don't pay enough. Also, I think it's very important to be open to new softwares and learn as many as you can so when a client only has one or the other, you are versed in both.

"No problem. I'll send it right over," is what you will be able to say.

With both softwares, you are able to import files directly into an email composition.

Which brings me to my next point.
Create a Gmail account.
COST = FREE

You're thinking, "Can't I just create any email account?"

Sure! You can do whatever you want. I prefer being able to use the apps that Google provides. Since Gmail, Drive, Sheets, Google Ads, and Youtube are all part of Google, it's extremely easy to navigate between them. Just a personal preference is all. After creating an email account, you can create a few accounts on websites where people are already looking for a freelancer.

Freelancing Websites:
Fiverr.com

UpWork.com
Guru.com
Craigslist.com
COST = FREE

I'll be honest, I haven't needed to put my work on there just yet but I always think about doing it just to have income from another angle. Even if it's a couple of gigs a month, that's a couple of gigs a month, right? The reason I mention these sites are because I have actually hired freelancers from them before. I've outsources some graphic design work, a few times, to a couple of freelancers. I've also hired someone to help edit this book on Upwork. These websites are good for outsourcing projects or getting hired by someone outsourcing their project.

I haven't had anyone hire me for an ad that I posted on Craigslist but I have definitely had success when it comes to submitting my work and setting up meetings. Sometimes it works, sometimes it doesn't. For instance, at the moment, I am in Massachusetts. People in MA are afraid to even use the site because they hear horror stories about "Craigslist Killers" or some stupid shit. I would highly recommend this site if you are in New York City or another major city because people actually post things in the cities. I have yet to find a gig in MA on here for a videographer that wasn't related to the porn industry, but I still use it to find cheap gear or equipment all the time. I bought my Native Instruments' Maschine from Craigslist. I even use it for purchasing used furniture when furnishing a new apartment.

I even used it to sell my lovely keyboard when I needed to pay rent.

That was a very sad day!

I use it to sell things often. I used it to sell my furniture when I couldn't move it all back to MA, from NYC, in the truck that I bought. I actually found my truck on Craigslist. I found a few apartments on Craigslist too. Be careful with this one because there are scams. In this particular instance, if it's too good to be true, it is. Trust me. Nobody is subletting their entire apartment while they are away on business in Africa and they ask you to send money for someone to deliver the key for a viewing. It's so pathetic what people will do. Just be careful. That being said, I have definitely found some apartments that were beautiful and the landlords were very, very nice people. I have used it when we were looking for a new roommate, and we found one. That didn't last long but we definitely found one. I am sure there are some good eggs out there.

Let's create an eBay account next.
COST = FREE

You should already have one, to be honest. I use that website to buy things more than any other website. It's really easy to set up an account to buy things and a little more involved when you are trying to sell products of your own. It's not overly complicated but I recommend creating a separate bank account that attaches to your eBay point of sale. The fees can catch you off guard. If you are selling on eBay, chances are you are trying to make money, not lose it in fees that haven't been paid.

I have personally used this site to buy Native Instruments' Komplete Kontrol. I used it to sell a couple of iPhones I had that were laying around and unlocked. I helped my friend sell her leftover supplements from a pyramid scheme that she was involved in. (She got out of it and had leftover products and wanted to make her money back. She did. Fast!) I've bought three cameras using eBay, and a couple of lenses as well. Right now, I have Beanie Babies from my childhood up for sale, and someone just bought one the other day.

I have bought more than I have sold on this site but I love everything about it. I usually try to only search for *"Buy Now"* things that have a low price and try and negotiate with them. It works. Especially if you can show them that the price they are asking for is absurd by sending links of the same product sold by someone else that's cheaper. I have used this to win bids as well but those are too stressful for me because I am not in control and I hate that. At the last second, someone will come in and press "bid" and you won't have time to bid again. It's not fun for someone who likes winning and negotiating.

I have sold headphones on there too. It's perfect for electronics. Seriously, they even give you a list of things that are best sellers on there. I have sold my leftover RAM from my old computer when I upgraded it. Also, I literally just searched through the things laying around that I haven't used in over six months to a year and listed over twenty items on my eBay account. It took me two days and now I wait for sales. Why not, right? Let the traffic and products do their own thing while you can go out and perform a service that pays more than a couple of dollars. When you return, it's almost like you made money while you were making money. Or maybe, you wake up to a notification saying that you sold an item. That is literally making money while you sleep. As you can see, I have used it quite often and to be quite honest with you, I can't even remember all the times I have used it. It's a game of patience here. I check for deals every week when I am in need of something. I prepare and see what the trending prices are and when they drop, BOOM, it's time to buy or negotiate.

Create a Paypal account.
COST = FREE

I fucking LOVE Paypal. Here's why: eBay and Paypal work very, very well together. You are able to pay your fees directly from your Paypal account. Paypal also ensures that you get what you are paying for. If not, they refund your money and charge the seller. Not many people know this but you no longer have to wait three days to transfer the money back to your checking account that is linked to it. You can convert the account to a business account and they will send you a business debit card in the mail. The card can be used at any location just like you would use a regular debit card. In fact, I just received my new one because they added the chip for even more security. I use Paypal for peace of mind when purchasing online. I use it to create little buttons with prices, so people can check out as soon as they click the link. It's easy to do but not many people know how. I like using it because I can transfer money back and forth between multiple Paypal accounts for free if I need to add money to my business accounts or pay myself from my business accounts. Their customer service is incredible and I've never not had my questions answered fully. There is an entire back end of Paypal for businesses. You can create invoices, buttons, HTML codes for your websites, shopping carts, and so much more.

Here is a "Pro Tip!" Each Paypal account needs its own bank

account attached to it. Here's the thing, you only need the account attached but you don't ever have to use the bank account if you just use the Paypal debit card instead of transferring funds from Paypal to your bank account. It's an added layer of security for those annoying monthly subscriptions that are always sucking you dry. Essentially, you can use it like I do and leave your profit in there when you're selling products or getting paid for services. Just don't give out *that* debit card number and the subscriptions will attack an empty bank account. Make sure your bank account has zero fees. Usually, with most software and app subscriptions, they notify you before they cancel your account, so you have time to transfer the exact amount you need to pay when *you* are ready, and never sooner. There's nothing worse than being broke as fuck, showing up to a cash register at a supermarket, trying to buy some food with your last $10.00, and it gets declined because a $9.99 subscription came out before you were able to eat for survival. Yes, it's happened to me on several occasions which is why I am giving you a heads up about paying yourself first and how to fully control who gets to see your money. Which brings me to the next point.

Download Cash App or Venmo
COST = FREE

There are a lot of apps that allow your friends to pay you instantly, as long as *they* linked *their* debit card up to a bank account. Cash App is one of those apps. I believe the more ways you can receive money, the easier it is for you to get paid. Would you agree? If I told you that I can pay you via Cash App, right now, but you only have a Paypal account, guess what? I have to send you a check because I don't have Paypal. Now you are waiting a week for me to write the check and another week for shipping. Instead, you should open as many avenues of payment as you can before you even start acquiring customers.

That's why I have Paypal, Cash App, and Venmo. Venmo is actually owned by Paypal at the moment. They're all very similar. My readers are probably very familiar with Cash App but what you may not know is, once again, you can get a debit card for that Cash App account so you don't have to wait a few days to see it in your bank account. It's also a good way to forget you have money sitting in another account if you leave it there. I love those kinds of surprises.

Oohh, shit!!! I forgot I got paid with this app.

It's like finding money in an old coat pocket just when you needed it most. What I have tried to do is to eliminate as many fees as I can while receiving and exchanging funds as fast as possible. Thanks to a great friend of mine, I found a great bank account without fees.

Capital One 360 checking accounts
COST = FREE

At the moment of writing this book, they are fee free. There are no overdraft fees and it's easy to set up online. I have at least three accounts with them. Some are set up just for Paypal accounts that are linked to eBay accounts, and some are for spending. Some are just to have in case I need to hold some money in an account where its debit card or routing numbers have not been handed out to any subscription services. FULL CONTROL. Remember that.

Side note, you can only open up three checking accounts with one Social Security number at this time. Try using a business EIN to open more if you need more. Don't quote me on this, but I think one business EIN can open up to 10 checking accounts. You are probably wondering why you would need so many but when you are trying to find the exact return on your investments while putting money aside for new equipment, it comes in handy. When you want to take vacations or trips around the world and you have all your spending, business, and personal combined, it's not a good idea. Also, I think it's a bit frowned upon by the IRS when you are claiming stupid shit on your taxes. Just saying. By having separate accounts, you can clearly show where and when money was coming and going while showing them what it was used for.

You'll need a smartphone.
COST = $300(+)

Personally, I love my iPhone but that's only because I love Apple products. It doesn't matter what phone you have as long as you can download apps, because you'll be downloading apps for all sorts of things. Like apps associated with your bank accounts. It's easy to log in and log out. I haven't gone to the bank for the longest time. The last time I went to the bank was with someone else who hasn't adapted to the times. Why would you stand in line to deposit a check when you can have it automatically deposited after you scan it with the app? You can transfer money back and forth between your accounts free of charge, right at the cash register and still be in full control of how much you need in your "spending account."

You'll also use the smartphone for other apps like Venmo and Cash App. Again, it's easy to check balances, receive payments, transfer money, and more. You'll need it to post on social media and interact with potential clients. It's great to be able to video chat with a client from anywhere when they have a question. You can use apps like Skype, Facetime, Snapchat, Facebook Messenger, etc. It's great for Youtube tutorials or Googling things when you are stumped. It's also great to watch or listen to content on Danna University!

#PLUG!

It's amazing when you get notifications from your online store when you sell an e-commerce product, or when you get notified of a payment being received. There's no reason for you to not already have a cell phone but some people don't, and I would challenge you to run a business without one and be successful. It's a great tool. Use it.

An external hard drive.
COST = $100 - $300

With the size of the files nowadays, you need an external hard drive. I recommend using a Glyph hard drive. I've never once had an issue with them losing my files, projects, or not appearing when I plug them in. If anything, the Glyph is so reliable that I found out one of my USB ports was no longer working. I thought it was the hard drive but I plugged it into another port in another computer, and it worked just fine. Come to find out, I had a broken USB port. Seriously, this is very important. In addition to the cloud apps that you may pay for, it's nice to have something physical in my opinion, to reference and use as your ultimate library.

I have three external hard drives on my desk as I write this. It's always a lovely feeling to me when I have maxed out a hard drive or come close to maxing one out. It means that I have been working so much that I need more space. That can't be a bad thing.

Just to give you as much detail as I can, I have two Glyphs and one My Book. The My Book is okay. It works. I have traveled with it on several occasions but it's definitely made me sick to my stomach when I was waiting for it to appear on my screen. It's happened a couple of times. My Book is a cheaper way to acquire more space but the reliability is not all there. One Glyph is a 3TB hard drive and the other is 2TB. I had the 2TB one first and nearly maxed it out right before a shoot. I had to upgrade and the 3TB was cheaper per GB after doing the math. I got a little geeky when I bought these. It was as if they were wholesaling GB space to me. I hope this helps.

Instagram and Facebook.
COST = FREE

You probably already have these but it's very important because they each have business accounts you can set up as well. You can turn a personal account into a business account and since Facebook owns Instagram, they integrate well with each other.

They also integrate well with website builders if you decide to market with all three. Facebook's pixel is a MUST have if you have a website and want to have even the slightest clue who your audience is. I won't waste your time when it comes to social media. You know how to use it better than I do. An app that a lot of people forget about, that most people have but lost their login credentials for it, is Skype.

Download Skype
COST = FREE

Skype is fantastic for sharing your screen with your clients when you want to show them a rough cut or rough draft of the design, etc. I use it to show my clients a rough edit of a commercial, music video, web series, or film. It's better than Zoom! By far!

Last but not least, the will to learn.
COST = FREE

If you don't want to learn, there's your first mistake. If you are willing to learn and make mistakes, you will succeed. If there are specific words you do not understand, Google them. Once you learn what those words mean, you'll stumble upon other terms or phrases that you do not understand. Google those! It's easy. At first, you'll spend months just Googling and researching phrases and terms. Once you start to get a grip on how the internet works and how to properly research (avoiding all the spam and junk articles) you'll be able to research much faster.

In turn, you'll be able to get back to hustling and working on a project while fully understanding it inside and out. You'll save time by noticing if a website is legit or not.

One tool that saves me time when I Google things from my computer is the "Tools" button as I search for something. You can adjust it to the most current article or an article posted on the topic within the last year or more. You can adjust it to pick the most popular one as well. Sometimes softwares and issues with the softwares have been fixed. You may Google an issue you're having and come across an article that states that the issue is not fixable but the date of the post was from 4 years ago. When you use the "Tools" tab, you can find out if someone recently had the problem or if they recently figured it out. It's amazing. It cuts straight to the chase.

If you have the stomach to handle being confused often and being patient enough to find the answer, it's all right there for you. The key is to learn these softwares as best as you can. The more you learn, the more you can charge. These are just examples or the softwares that I use on a weekly basis, if not daily. The softwares are not as important as the techniques. If you can learn how to use a free software that changes the color of images and you can manipulate layers, masks, and whatever else, you may not need to use Photoshop. However, there are benefits to using softwares that have become the standard. The tutorials online are everywhere, because everyone uses them. (I'll even have a Photoshop course as part of Danna University in the near future. By the time you read this, the course may already be up on www.DannaUniversity.com.)

I have tried the cheap or free route before and it's even harder to learn because not a lot of people want to make tutorials on how to use it. I prefer Premiere Pro for video editing, but you can use Final Cut Pro X and people love that. The process and techniques are still similar. They're designed for video editing. They both chop up clips in a timeline. They both have volume adjustment and color adjustment panels. What I'm saying is, use what works best for you. You may use one over the other just because you already have it on your computer or you like the interface and colors better. I don't care what you use. Seriously, just learn and try and master whatever it is you are learning to use.

Let's tally it up and show you the cost to start a business with some of the best tools on the market that can help you become your own boss!

ITEM	COST	NOTES
Computer	$2,000	You should already have this
Adobe x 12 Months	$648/year	
Internet x 12 Months	$600/year	Cafe has this for FREE
Dropbox x 12 Months	$120/year	Don't need it right away
Smartphone	$300	You should already have this
External Hard Drive	$300	Beyond worth it
TOTAL	**$3,968**	

I didn't include the things that would be free to create or set up in the chart above. Can you believe it will only cost you $3,968.00 to start freelancing? To be honest, it should cost you way less than that because you should already have a smartphone and a computer. Maybe you already have an external hard drive as well. It's crazy. I've never done the math for this but I am happy I did it for you. I just had to find this shit out on my own without anyone walking me through it. I can't say I did it all on my own because I have to give credit to all the YouTubers that I've had the pleasure of learning from over the years.

I have to point out that I did not include the fees for creating a company and here's why. I do not recommend starting a company for the services you provide until you know that you can sell your services and want to take the next step. Even then, I would be hesitant. Unless you are going to do it correctly--which most people online will not understand or show you how to do-- then you will just waste your money. Until you are working very often, just freelance for a while and keep track of your receipts.

PAY YOUR TAXES

You are going to have to file a 1099-misc now. If you are reading this and you already have a job, then you will have to file both a W-2 and a 1099-misc. However, I do recommend working with friends and family at first and having them gift you money or pay you in cash to start out. It's tax-free that way. If they aren't paying for a service or product, you're doing them a favor and they can "tip" you if they want. See what I am saying? Who can track tips? Only at the beginning. Don't think this will work when you start to write off equipment and expenses as a freelancer. They'll want to know how much money you had coming in and where it went as soon as you can. All I am saying is that creating a business right off the bat will show the government that you are about to pay taxes because you are about to sell and make a profit. Don't waste your time. What if you experiment with a couple of different gigs and don't like any of them and you already created a company for each one? I said this before, it's just a piece of paper. Don't worry about it until it's absolutely necessary. You'll know when that is.

BUILDING YOUR
OWN WEBSITE

When the time comes and you have learned how to do a couple of things that you might be able to get paid for, keep doing it. Don't worry about building a website right off the bat. Now, you will need to know how and I suggest that you use a company called www.Wix.com. The reason I have said Wix is because I use them and I love them. They have their limitations but since I started using them back in 2013, they have improved in so many ways. In fact, you can actually use code to build your website with them too, if you know how to code. That's a recent update. There are a host of website builders that are drag and drop for people that don't know how to code. Squarespace is another. This could change, but right now, Wix is offering a free domain with the free website builder. It's an amazing way to get familiar with a software while not having to pay astronomical fees before you launch products or services. If you don't have anything to sell or aren't making money yet, why would you want to or even be able to pay for a software just to learn how to use it?

In my opinion, it's awesome that they do this because it's free to teach yourself how to use their software. Once you learn it, you need to pay to add your own custom domain but you can create an entire website before you even get to that point. The best part is, you can edit it and completely destroy all your fuck ups while you're not on a subscription-based payment plan. I'm sure other builders do that same thing or have a trial period but for me, off the top of my head, this is the only one that has an unlimited trial period. Pretty sweet right?

22

I HOPE THIS HELPED

I don't know how authors stop writing after a few hundred pages! Maybe I will have to figure out how to cut down the size of my book and only keep the golden nuggets. I definitely feel like I touched on a few points that needed to be discussed at length which may call for more books to be written. The main thing I wanted to make sure I did with this book, was to allow you to get to know me and where I came from. Hoping you could relate, I attempted to give you lessons that I have learned through trial and error over the years. Have I motivated you to go out, experiment, fail, learn, and teach others from your lessons?

Please, from this day forward, focus on investing in yourself. Follow your gut and make sure you love what you are doing. It really doesn't matter what you decide to do. Try to balance out your life with rewarding yourself for hustling and try to outdo yourself the next time you grind. Remember, until now, I was not considered an author. I stuck with what I believed I should be doing and found out that I thoroughly enjoy writing books and unleashing all the shit bouncing around in my brain on a daily basis. You too, have an author inside of you. Use your story to create a product or service that will help others. It's very fulfilling to know that this book could change one person's life. It's even more fulfilling to know it could change two lives. By writing this book and publishing it myself, I stayed true to what I am committed to accomplishing by creating a product that only has to be created one time. For the rest of my life, I will be making money and helping from the ideas I had rattling around upstairs. Can you believe that? One time! I sat down and just busted my ass.

Of course, it wasn't all hustle, there were (and still are) some days where I just sit and play Madden for half the day. That is exactly the point I want to get across. Hustle, but don't forget that happiness does not come from hustle alone. Happiness will be found with balance and deciding to be happy. Whatever your situation. I could be a miserable bastard and complain about my current living situation until the cows come home. What good would that do me? I channeled my frustration and anger into a couple of softwares that created a book for me.

Use whatever you have around as inspiration and run with it. Whether it is a situation you intend to remove yourself from or something you just want to make better, use it as fuel. Don't let anyone box you into what they think *your* life should look like. Prove them wrong. If you have doubters and negative people around you, focus on being introverted for a little while and see how much you accomplish without telling people what you are working on.

I know it can be scary. It can be extremely scary to not know where your next paycheck is coming from. At the same time, you will also feel something that very few can say they feel when they wake up in the morning. It's that feeling of freedom. Don't worry about shit that is out of your control. Focus on what you can control and perform at the best of your abilities. Remember, you're in this for the long haul and you aren't going to see immediate results. Play the long game! Labels are limits! Don't be afraid to experiment and fail. All the lessons and stories in this book have come from failure and curiosity. Don't let anyone tell you that you can't do something. Don't tell anyone they can't do something. Remain positive because the tough times never last and there is always something to be grateful for.

Despite my situation, living in my Brother's Girlfriend's Mother's house, with them, has been an experience of a lifetime. I know it's not permanent and I know that I would have never been able to write this book if I didn't have this roof over my head for $100.00 a month. Is the house full of negative energy? Yes! Is it stressful to know that everyone you live with thinks you should get a real job? Of course. Somehow, I channeled all that into this book in hopes that you will know that you are not alone and you can accomplish anything you want in life.

Believe in yourself because it will be A VERY LONG TIME before other people believe in you. Don't forget to relax and reward yourself along the way. Last but not least, I left the boss that was paying me $20 per hour, for work I had no interest in doing. A few months later, I was hired by him to take photos of the bars that I used to manage for him. I ended up increasing my hourly wage by 300% because I work for myself. He paid me a wage that I was willing to work for and I was able to do what I really enjoyed for a few hours. Funny how the tables turn. You CAN do the same! Go get it! ;)

For more information or if you have questions about anything related to this book, please do not hesitate to reach out!

Visit www.DannaUniversity.com for everything entrepreneur!

"Love you guys! Thank you for reading this long ass book. Remember, Stick With Me, Kid. You'll Go Places!"

www.ingramcontent.com/pod-product-compliance
Lightning Source LLC
Chambersburg PA
CBHW031948070426
42453CB00006BA/137